THIRD EDITION

RECLAIMING YOUTH AT RISK

Futures of Promise

Larry K. Brendtro | Martin Brokenleg | Steve Van Bockern

Solution Tree | Press

a division of
Solution Tree

555 North Morton Street
Bloomington, IN 47404
800.733.6786 (toll free) / 812.336.7700
FAX: 812.336.7790

email: info@SolutionTree.com
SolutionTree.com

Printed in the United States of America

Library of Congress Control Number: 2019001922

Solution Tree
Jeffrey C. Jones, CEO
Edmund M. Ackerman, President

Solution Tree Press
President and Publisher: Douglas M. Rife
Associate Publisher: Sarah Payne-Mills
Art Director: Rian Anderson
Managing Production Editor: Kendra Slayton
Senior Production Editor: Todd Brakke
Content Development Specialist: Amy Rubenstein
Proofreader: Evie Madsen
Text and Cover Designer: Abigail Bowen
Editorial Assistant: Sarah Ludwig

Circle of Courage art by George Blue Bird

Table of Contents

About the Authors

Larry K. Brendtro, PhD, is professor emeritus of special education at Augustana University and directs the Resilience Academy providing research, publications, and training. He is a licensed psychologist with broad experience in youth development. As president of Starr Commonwealth in Michigan, he developed alternative schools and treatment programs. He served thirteen years on the U.S. Coordinating Council on Juvenile Justice and Delinquency Prevention. His publications are available in several languages, and he trains professionals worldwide.

He holds a doctorate from the University of Michigan and taught at the University of Illinois and The Ohio State University.

Martin Brokenleg, EdD, is professor emeritus of Native American Studies at Augustana University and was director of Native Ministries and a professor at the Vancouver School of Theology at the University of British Columbia. Dr. Brokenleg has provided training and consultation throughout North America and abroad including work with Indigenous peoples from many nations.

He holds a doctorate in psychology and is a graduate of the Episcopal Divinity School. He has extensive counseling experience in the areas of cultural trauma and substance abuse. He is an enrolled member of the Rosebud Sioux Tribe and resides in Victoria, British Columbia, Canada.

Steve Van Bockern, EdD, is a professor of education at Augustana University and hosts the annual Reclaiming Youth seminars. With experience as a teacher and principal at the elementary and secondary levels, he consults with schools and alternative and special education programs in many nations. His publications include the book *Schools That Matter,* which applies the reclaiming concepts to meet growth needs of all students. He and his wife Sarah, a school psychologist, have conducted strength-based assessments with challenging students and have been expert witnesses in juvenile court proceedings.

To learn more about the authors' work, visit Reclaiming Youth at Risk (https://reclaimingyouthatrisk.org).

To book Larry K. Brendtro, Martin Brokenleg, or Steve Van Bockern for professional development, contact pd@SolutionTree.com.

About the Artist

George Blue Bird is a Lakota artist who grew up on the Pine Ridge Indian Reservation in South Dakota. He began serving a life sentence for an alcohol-related homicide in his early twenties. When his art was published in the previous edition of this book, we presented George with the first copy at a ceremony in the prison school where he taught art to fellow prisoners.

Displaying his drawings, he noted "This is a medicine wheel. Tribal people use the circle to show that all of life must be in balance and that we all must be connected to one another. The four colors—black, white, red, and yellow—stand for the four directions, and for the four races. We should all live in harmony, part of the same circle."

Describing the drawing for Belonging, George said, "I read in the manuscript that every child needs some adult who is crazy about him, so I drew myself dancing with my son, White Buffalo. I haven't seen him since he was two months old—he would be six years old now."

George showed the art for Mastery. "I painted myself as a boy with my grandfather who taught me to shoot a bow and arrow. Grandfather said, 'You'll probably miss most of the time, but that doesn't matter. What matters is that you always do the best that you can.'"

To portray Independence, George displayed the art of a youth sitting in thought atop a mountain. "I painted a youth on a vision quest. In this rite of passage, a young person goes out to live alone to discover what his path in life will be."

The art showing Generosity was displayed last. George pointed to the grandmother giving soup to hungry children. He explained that the test of Generosity was to treat others as relatives. "In my Lakota language, we often say *Mitakuye Oyasin*, which means 'we are all relatives.'"

A color poster of George Blue Bird's art is available with proceeds going to the George Blue Bird Defense Fund.[1] A biography of the life of George Blue Bird has been published by the Sioux Falls *Argus Leader*.[2] George Blue Bird has authored a chapter on Indigenous persons in the prison system.[3]

Preface

When the three of us conceived this project as faculty members at Augustana University, we could not envision that this "little green book" would set the stage for contributions by colleagues worldwide, and we would like to acknowledge those contributions.

The philosophy of reclaiming youth sparked the annual Black Hills Seminars, initially hosted by Fred Tully of the Children's Home Society. These seminars now continue at Augustana University in Sioux Falls, South Dakota, where the authors of this book have served on the faculty. For two decades, the *Reclaiming* journal was co-edited by Nicholas J. Long and Larry K. Brendtro, and its successor is the online journal *Thriving* edited by Mark Freado. Other long-time members of the Reclaiming Youth staff include Wendy Beukelman, Susan Buus, Charity Helleson, and Janna Brendtro.

Historically, the reclaiming youth movement has roots in the work of Fritz Redl and colleagues at the University of Michigan. Starr Commonwealth became a laboratory for developing these approaches under the successive leadership of Larry Brendtro, Arlin Ness, Martin Mitchell, and Elizabeth Carey. The strength-based movement was advanced through research by Erik Laursen on Positive Peer Culture and Robert Foltz on the neuroscience of positive youth development. Frank Fescer has continued this relational tradition through the Life Space Crisis Intervention program. Cathann Kress established the Circle of Courage as the essential goals of 4-H, the largest youth development organization in the United States. James Anglin of the University of Victoria in British Columbia conducted research on relational strategies for youth showing pain-based behavior. Ken McCluskey and faculty of the University of Winnipeg provide training and publications on trauma and resilience. We also acknowledge our late colleague J. C. Chambers who shared skills at connecting with youth in *The Art of Kid Whispering.*[1]

Canadian anthropologist Inge Bolin described Indigenous "cultures of respect" as expressions of Circle of Courage values. These principles were linked to positive psychology by Christopher Peterson and to social and emotional learning by Linda Lantieri. John Seita secured Kellogg Foundation grants for a new model of strength-based assessment. Extending this work to Indigenous populations were Adrienne Brant James and Tammy Lunday of Turtle Island Learning Circle. Larry Wilke brought the Circle of Courage to First Nations students in Canada. Educators are now the largest group of professionals using these approaches which Nancy Koehler and Vikki Hennard first piloted in Michigan.

The International Child and Youth Care Network—led by Brian Gannon, Thom Garfat, and Leon Fulcher—disseminated this philosophy worldwide. Lesley du Toit brought the Circle of Courage to South Africa to serve young people at risk during the administration of Nelson Mandela. Howard Bath and Diana Boswell piloted training across Australia, which is now continued by Allambi Youth Services and by Tim McDonald of Western Australia. Diane Guild and Deborah Espiner created the first Circle of Courage schools in New Zealand and developed a curriculum for building family strengths. Lloyd and Anthea Martin train youth workers in New Zealand, Australia, and the Pacific Islands.

In Europe, Beate Kreisle forged a network of German organizations using the Circle of Courage and Positive Peer Culture. Christoph Steinebach and colleagues from Zurich University have linked these principles to resilience science and positive psychology.

Franky D'Oosterlinck has established training networks in Holland and Belgium. John Digney and Max Smart provide leadership to reclaiming youth training in the United Kingdom and Ireland. Arlene Kee and Stephen Hughes have developed programs in Northern Ireland, while Ceri May is employing this model in England.

These are but a few contributions by inspired professionals who move toward youth at risk while others keep their distance. In the words of a young person: "You can tell the staff here really like their jobs because they want to help kids. They constantly are thinking about us—how to meet our needs, how this can be a better place to make us successful."

Introduction

The values of the Circle of Courage evolved over thousands of years in cultures that deeply revere children. We shared this knowledge within the publication of the first edition of *Reclaiming Youth at Risk* with illustrations by Lakota artist George Blue Bird. For this wholly revised third edition, we re-examined and restructured our approach to the reclaiming model to provide an even more comprehensive understanding of how Native science and the current research into brain-based learning can function together to support and reclaim our most troubled youth.

Indeed, the reclaiming model is a synergy of Indigenous wisdom, perspectives of youth-work pioneers, and leading-edge research on resilience, neuroscience, and positive youth development. Samuel R. Slavson first used the word *reclaiming* in connection with youth at risk. He believed their most basic needs were to trust and be trusted. Receiving love is not enough—young people need opportunities to give love as well.[1] The first systematic study of the reclaiming process came from Israel, which has a rich history of serving displaced youth. Martin Wolins and Yochanan Wozner defined *reclaiming* as meeting the needs of both the young person and society.[2]

Our book title uses the person-first label ***youth** at risk*, which refers to environmental hazards that disrupt development. In contrast, the common use of ***at-risk** youth* implies the blame lies with the young person. But humans are all are at risk, and it is our human bonds that enable us to survive and thrive. Such is the message of the sub-title, *Futures of Promise*.

This book is grounded in the Circle of Courage model of resilience and positive youth development based on Native American values of Belonging, Mastery, Independence, and Generosity. When the circle is complete, humans live in harmony and balance. When the circle is broken, discouragement ensues, with youth being particularly at risk of becoming lost. But they can be *reclaimed*.

This book's structure is straightforward. Chapter 1 explores important cultural and biosocial values that the Circle of Courage represents as well as some enduring truths about the necessary con-silience of thought and ideas necessary to reclaim youth at risk. Chapter 2 fully introduces the Circle of Courage and the impor-tance its values have in reclaiming traumatized youth. Chapter 3 explores the seeds of discouragement that place youth at risk when their Circle of Courage is broken. Chapters 4 through 7 each explore in detail one of the four core values of the Circle of Courage, how each can be broken and the approaches you can use to understand and mend it. Finally, chapter 8 concludes the book by reflecting on the journey of reclaiming youth at risk through the lens of resilience, recovery, and healing.

By understanding the relationship of Circle of Courage values with the challenges youth experience when those values are absent from their lives, you can apply the reclaiming model to your practice and help the youth you serve to discover their most promising futures.

CHAPTER 1

Enduring Truths

We are drowning in information, while starving for wisdom.

—*E. O. Wilson*[1]

Harvard researcher E. O. Wilson says complexity is overwhelming every field of study.[2] Scientists entrenched in silos of knowledge churn out mountains of data that are inaccessible, incomprehensible, or irrelevant. This knowledge explosion is exacerbated as anyone can now use an internet-connected device to google *resilience* and *children* yielding millions of hits. Literally, we suffer from data overload.

Amidst this flood of information, practitioners face mandates to adopt *evidence-based* approaches in education, treatment, and youth development.[3] But as child psychiatrist John Werry of Auckland University notes, so-called evidence-based interventions often have *statistical* significance yet are *insignificant* in the real world of practice.[4] Thus, instead of preoccupation with *evidence-based practices*, we believe the goal of any practitioner tasked with developing and supporting youth at risk is to identify *evidence-based principles*.

Searching for Solutions

How do we select the core principles that can guide our work with children and families? The solution is *consilience,* a term 19th century British scholar William Whewell coined. Trained in three professions—(1) science, (2) architecture, (3) and theology—he was intrigued to discover connections among these dissimilar fields. He observes that findings from separate disciplines jump together to identify powerful simple truths.[5]

Wilson reintroduced the concept of consilience when he observed that hyperspecialization obscures the reality that there is a "unity of knowledge."[6] Consilience links findings from different fields to discover simpler universal principles. Simple does not mean simplistic; as Einstein once said, if you can't explain your theory to a six-year-old, you probably don't understand it yourself.[7] Figure 1.1 shows three essential sources of truth—(1) values, (2) experience, and (3) science—which form the evidence base for this book. The following sections examine each of these sources.

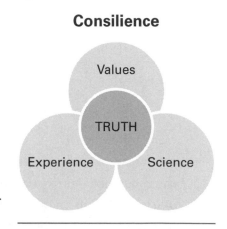

Figure 1.1: Sources of evidence.

Values: What Matters Most

Values are rooted in both culture and biology. Throughout most of human evolution, people lived in Indigenous societies which we describe as *cultures of respect*, a shared humanity toward others. The Zulu language calls this worldview *Ubuntu*. Across millennia, humans survived and thrived in egalitarian communities which shared core values.[8] Children and elders are held in great respect, the entire village is involved in raising the young, and the leaders are servants of the people.

Cultural values determine how society rears and educates children. The lens for our discussion is grounded in values that emerged over thousands of years in traditional societies that deeply revere children. Our focus is on the values of the Circle of Courage: Belonging, Mastery, Independence, and Generosity.

> *In our every deliberation, we must consider the impact of our decisions on the next seven generations.*
>
> *—Iroquois Confederacy Maxim*

Biosocial values are the brain-based motivations that shape human behavior across cultures and throughout the lifespan. Philosopher Mortimer J. Adler observes that not all values are relative; absolute values are those tied to universal human needs.[9] By the design of their DNA, humans have inborn drives for Attachment, Achievement, Autonomy, and Altruism. These brain-based needs align with the Circle of Courage values.

Developmental needs of children are universal since these are tied to the human genome. Yet societies place different priorities on certain values. For example, Western culture emphasizes individualism while many other civilizations place more emphasis on group belonging.[10] Those cultures which attend to all basic needs produce healthier and happier children.[11] These form the foundation for creating schools and communities where children thrive.

Experience: Practical Wisdom

Another source of knowledge comes from life experience; for example, the contributions of pioneers in education and youth work. A powerful voice for reclaiming youth was Janusz Korczak, who established orphanage schools for Jewish street children in Warsaw.[12] A champion of youth empowerment, Korczak authored twenty books, from his earliest *Children of the Street* penned in 1901 to his final *Ghetto Diary*, written in 1942 while living under Nazi occupation.[13] Believing that children were *citizens in embryo*, he gave young people a voice in running their school. Moral development psychologist Lawrence Kohlberg considered Korczak as the exemplar of a *just and caring community*.[14]

Practice expertise is a recognized source of evidence-based practice in the profession of psychology.[15] Our discussion also draws from the wisdom of pioneers in youth work in the Western tradition.[16] These individuals challenge authoritarian systems of education and child-rearing in Eurocentric cultures.

Science is nothing more than a refinement of everyday thinking.
                                                    —Albert Einstein[17]

Client expertise recognizes that those we serve are the ultimate authorities on their own lives. Democratic values call for empowering the voice of youth, and parents are literally lifespan experts on their children. Further, many professionals in this field bring unique perspectives as former youth at risk themselves.[18]

Zulu sociologist Herbert Vilakazi further notes that elaborate knowledge about child-rearing predates Western science.[19] He describes how traditional African men and women, particularly the women, were consummate psychologists with sophisticated understanding of child development. Researchers have observed these patterns in Indigenous cultures worldwide.

Child-rearing in traditional tribal cultures focuses on meeting the developmental needs of children.[20] Indigenous people rear respectful, responsible children without resorting to harsh punishment. In contrast, Western parenting and education is tethered to obedience models of discipline. With the advent of democracy, inspired reformers advocated for progressive approaches in education and youth work. We tap their practice wisdom throughout this book.

Science: Two Worlds of Knowledge

The traditional view sees science as a product of Western civilization. A more informed understanding is that humans have always been applied scientists, searching to make sense of their world. A course correction is underway as experts in a variety of fields recognize the broad scope of Indigenous knowledge.

Indigenous science (which we also refer to as *Native science*) encompasses a little-explored trove of knowledge from *homo sapiens*—the Latin designation for *wise man*. The highly developed brain of this species and the vast knowledge it produced predated Western science.[21] Native science describes the relationship of humans with nature, not only the way the world works but also the way to live in harmony.[22]

Let us put our minds together to see what kind of life we can build for our children.

—Sitting Bull[23]

Modern science focuses on empirical observations and experiments. Historian of science Steven Shapin quips, "There was no such thing as a scientific revolution, and this is a book about it."[24] The notion of such a revolution ignores the rich history of ancient thought. Consilience taps both Indigenous and Western science.

Native peoples acquired profuse knowledge by carefully observing their world and transmitting their discoveries through oral history. The authors of the *Encyclopedia of American Indian Contributions to the World* describe their work as mere brushstrokes of twenty-five thousand years of Native thought and creativity.[25]

With perspectives spanning generations, Native people had a holistic worldview that cannot be gained from brief isolated research studies. Western science seeks value-free knowledge by measuring cause-and-effect links between isolated variables. Indigenous science takes a relational and spiritual worldview of living in harmony with others and nature.[26]

Drawing on his Native American heritage, Harvard psychologist Joseph P. Gone describes the collision between competing mandates for *evidence-based practices* and *cultural competence*.[27] We cannot solve the problems of modern youth—drugs and alcohol, gangs and violence—utilizing narrow empirically based interventions. Instead, as educator David G. Blumenkrantz proposes, two million years of human evolution is the ultimate clinical trial for providing cultural wisdom that ensures survival.[28]

John Stuart Mill observes that the most original thinkers are those who thoroughly know what their predecessors already thought.[29] In this book, we seek to rediscover the maps our forbearers used as we prepare to sail away from conventional shores. This will be a transcultural journey employing the wisdom of youth-work pioneers in Western society as well as the untapped heritage of Indigenous perspectives of education and child-rearing. These theories of practice chart a course for claiming and reclaiming our youth.

Identifying Universal Needs

Long before modern science, Indigenous peoples used planful strategies to nurture respectful and responsible children. In Lakota culture, people called children *sacred beings*; the Maori word for child means *gift of God*; and in Africa, the Ibu word for child means *what wonders has God wrought*. These concepts arose from cultures that deeply cherished children.

What I have called the basic needs are probably common to all mankind and are therefore shared values.

—*Abraham H. Maslow*[30]

Our original research on the Circle of Courage principles largely drew from accounts of child-rearing and education in Native American cultures, such as those from Dakota physician scholar Charles A. Eastman, Lakota Chief and philosopher Luther Standing Bear, and anthropologist and educator Ella Deloria, aunt of noted Native author, Vine Deloria Jr. That research identifies four key values (the cultural values we listed previously) that permeated Native culture.

1. **Belonging (relationships of trust):** *I am loved.*
2. **Mastery (opportunities for learning):** *I can succeed.*
3. **Independence (building responsibility):** *I control my life.*
4. **Generosity (helping others):** *I have a purpose for my life.*

A growing body of research from the Western tradition validates these principles.[31] Junei Li and Megan M. Julian describe *developmental relationships* as the *active ingredient* in the success of all interventions with youth at risk.[32] Their definition draws from the following four descriptors of Urie Bronfenbrenner's classic research.[33] These correspond to Circle of Courage values and biosocial needs.

1. A strong emotional bond (Attachment, Belonging)
2. Increasingly complex tasks (Achievement, Mastery)
3. Power shifts to the learner (Autonomy, Independence)
4. Reciprocity of relationships (Altruism, Generosity)

Ironically, most efforts to improve schools and youth programs target inactive ingredients (such as incentives and high-stakes testing) which fail to produce powerful effects. Reinforcement, competition, and behavior control do not create lasting results.[34]

Although thousands of variables have some conceivable effect on life outcomes, there are a small number of key variables that produce powerful growth and change. Suniya S. Luthar reviewed five decades of research and concludes "resilience rests fundamentally on relationships."[35]

Using the principle of consilience, William C. Jackson surveys research on the Circle of Courage, positive youth development (https://youthpower.org), and childhood socialization.[36] Across many different models, four common themes emerge. While researchers

use different terms, most were synonyms for biosocial needs and
Circle of Courage values (see table 1.1).

Table 1.1: Consilience of Research on Positive Youth Development

Biosocial Needs	Attachment	Achievement	Autonomy	Altruism
Circle of Courage	Belonging	Mastery	Independence	Generosity
Hierarchy of Needs	Belongingness	Esteem	Self-actualization	Self-transcendence
Self-Esteem	Significance	Competence	Power	Virtue
Teaching Family	Relationships	Skills	Empowerment	Spirituality
Resilient Brains	Attachment	Mastery motivation	Self-efficacy	Spirituality and purpose

Jackson cites dozens of studies that identify factors matching the biosocial needs for Attachment, Achievement, Autonomy, and Altruism.
A prominent example was Abraham H. Maslow's final hierarchy of
human needs, which includes the added level self-transcendence.[37]
We find similar descriptors in Stanley Coopersmith's classic studies
on self-esteem,[38] the Boys Town Teaching-Family Model,[39] and Ann
Masten's research on the resilient brain.[40]

A review of research in the *Handbook of Social and Emotional
Learning* identifies the Circle of Courage as presaging other models
of positive youth development.[41] Bonnie Benard reviewed fifteen
studies of resilience and identifies common factors of social competence, problem solving, autonomy, and purpose.[42] Chris Peterson
analyzed positive psychology strengths and finds four dimensions
akin to the Circle of Courage.[43] Cathann Kress and 4-H researchers adopted the Circle of Courage as the *4-H Essentials of Youth
Development*. Kress notes that Tuft University researchers studied

4-H programs and renamed the Circle of Courage principles as *connection, confidence, competence, character*, and *caring*.[44]

Beyond our four biosocial needs, humans, like other creatures, have primitive brainstem programs for *approach* and *avoidance*—seeking pleasure, preventing pain.[45] While coercive discipline manipulates pain and pleasure to control behavior, the following brain programs are essential to well-being.

- *Avoidance* is tied to surviving and seeking *safety*, while *approach* is tied to thriving and seeking *adventure*. [46]
- *Safety* is a pillar of trauma prevention and treatment,[47] and young brains thrive on adventure.[48]

Human brains link pain and pleasure with biosocial values. Attachment, Achievement, Autonomy, and Altruism are inherently rewarding, while deprivation of these is painful. For example, children express joy at attachment and pain at separation. These basic psychological needs are essential for positive development and well-being.[49]

Across thousands of years, traditional cultural values have been grounded in the biosocial needs of children. Canadian anthropologist Inge Bolin has spent her career studying Indigenous Quechua children in Highland Peru. Living at fifteen thousand feet above sea level in the Andes, they grow up in a culture of respect.[50] Bolin describes how these children are immersed in Circle of Courage values.

- *Belonging* is ensured. Children are taught that loneliness is the saddest of experiences, so they should make certain that all are included.
- *Mastery* is seen in children's eagerness to learn and achieve. Yet they never flaunt their superiority but share their skills with one another.

- *Independence* is developed from earliest years as children receive important tasks. Anger with force is unknown and children are never harshly punished.

- *Generosity* is the foundation of respect. All children contribute to the community by helping the elderly and caring for younger children.

For five hundred years, these traditional values have been under attack on all continents as colonial forces subjugated Indigenous peoples. Schools became the primary means for acculturating the conquered. In Australia, it was the *Stolen Generations* removed from their families and trained to be servants to the settlers.[51] Europeans enslaved Africans to colonial masters or sold them into slavery. Although Indigenous peoples had accumulated rich knowledge about rearing respectful, responsible children, conquering powers cast this aside. Chapter 2, "The Circle of Courage," reclaims this Native wisdom.

CHAPTER 2
The Circle of Courage

Be it for now or a hundred years from now, or a thousand—so long as the race of humanity shall survive—the Indian keeps his gift for us all.

—John Collier[1]

When professionals find they are expected to build positive cultures in schools and youth-serving organizations, they are often perplexed. Even anthropologists who study cultures are never expected to create them. What could constitute the core of shared values, the unifying theme of such a culture? When we ask our university students to list what they believe to be the preeminent values in contemporary society, the prominent mainstay is "success" as defined by wealth, power, and materialism. Clearly, we have to look somewhere else to find a value base appropriate for claiming and reclaiming our youth.

Traditional Native American approaches to child-rearing challenge both European assumptions of child-rearing and the narrow perspectives of many psychological theories. Refined over tens of thousands of years of civilization and preserved in oral traditions, this knowledge is little known outside these tribal groups.

Until the early 20th century, the rich heritage of child-rearing among Indigenous peoples received scant attention from anthropologists.[2] However, in 1925, psychiatrist Carl Jung visited Taos Pueblo, and his encounter with an elder, Ochwiay Biano, shaped his subsequent writings.[3] Further, in 1938, two noted psychologists, Abraham H. Maslow and Erik H. Erikson, who studied Native child-rearing, strongly influenced contemporary theories of developmental psychology.

As his biographer, Edward Hoffman, describes, Abraham Maslow originally believed that *power* was the primary human motivation and that his extensive studies of the Northern Blackfoot in Alberta, Canada, upended this view.[4] Their culture was oriented around Generosity instead of dominance and wealth. Maslow estimated that 90 percent of the population were emotionally secure and thriving compared with perhaps 5–10 percent in Western society. In later years, Maslow revisited the Blackfoot and observed how the boarding school tradition had upended their culture.

Erikson studied Sioux (Lakota) child-rearing on the Pine Ridge Indian Reservation in South Dakota, and later with the Yurok tribe on the Pacific Coast of northern California. He was impressed that adults carefully nurtured each child's needs, which laid the foundation for Generosity as the outstanding virtue.[5] Yet, the Lakota were struggling to deal with Western influences while remaining committed to traditional values. Throughout the late 19th and early 20th centuries, Charles Eastman described this dilemma as *living in two worlds*.[6] Or as Native American psychologist Joseph Gone cleverly quips, "We never was happy living like a Whiteman."[7]

The Europeans who colonized Indigenous societies worldwide saw them as primitive, having little to offer a modern society. Yet, Native peoples possessed rich wisdom that immigrants to North America might well have adopted. Instead, missionaries and educators set out to "civilize" these young "savages" with an unquestioned belief in the superiority of Western approaches to education and child-rearing. Typically, this meant removing children from families and placing them in militaristic boarding schools.[8] Forbidden to speak their own language under penalty of severe whippings, colonial educators deliberately stripped away their supposedly inferior Indian identity.[9] "Kill the Indian to save the man" was the battle cry of these educators. Generations of such cultural intrusion have left deep scars of alienation on Indigenous peoples worldwide.

Native philosophies represent what is perhaps the most effective holistic system of positive youth development ever envisioned. These approaches emerged from cultures where children were sacred, and the central purpose of life was to meet their needs. Modern child-development research is only now reaching the point where it understands, validates, and replicates this holistic approach.[10]

The number four has sacred meaning to Native people who see the person as standing in a circle surrounded by the four directions. As shown in figure 2.1 and figure 2.2 (page 16), Lakota Sioux artist George Blue Bird portrays this philosophy of child development in the medicine wheel and art.[11] We propose Belonging, Mastery, Independence, and Generosity as the central values for education and youth work. We believe the philosophy embodied in this Circle of Courage is not only a cultural belonging of Native peoples but for all the world's children.

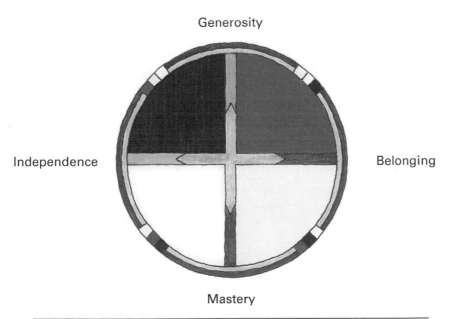

Figure 2.1: Circle of Courage values in a Native American medicine wheel.

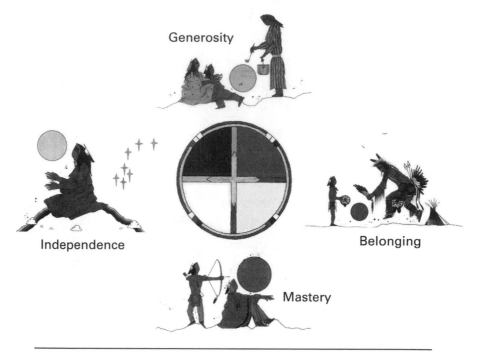

Generosity

Independence

Belonging

Mastery

Figure 2.2: Native American art depicting the Circle of Courage values.

The Spirit of Belonging

The pioneering American psychiatrist Karl Menninger contends that many children desperately pursue *artificial belongings* because families, schools, and communities do not fulfill their need to belong. A secure sense of belonging requires relationships with caring and supporting adults.[12]

> *Be related, somehow, to everyone you know.*
>
> —*Ella Deloria*[13]

In traditional Native society, it was the duty of all adults to serve as teachers for younger persons. Child-rearing was not just the province of biological parents, but children received nurturing within a larger circle of significant others. From the earliest days of life, all children experienced a network of caring adults. Standing Bear observed that each child belongs both to a certain family and to the band; wherever the child strayed, he or she was at home, for all claimed relationship:

> The days of my infanthood and childhood were spent in sur-
> roundings of love and care. In manner, gentleness was my
> mother's outstanding characteristic. Never did she, nor any of
> my caretakers, ever speak crossly to me or scold me for failures
> or shortcomings.[14]

Kinship in tribal settings was not strictly a matter of biological relationships. The ultimate test was behavior, not blood; you belonged if you acted like you belonged. Tribes invented relationships for persons who were left out so that everyone would feel included in a circle of relatives.[15]

Children learned to see themselves as related to virtually all with whom they had regular contact.[16] In Indigenous cultures worldwide, the elderly were grandparents, while aunts and uncles shared the status with biological parents as mothers and fathers.

Treating others as related was a powerful social value that transformed human relationships. Drawing them into one's circle motivated one to show respect and concern and to live with a minimum of friction and a maximum of goodwill.[17] Many Native peoples have a soft-spoken manner which results from a worldview that all should be treated with respect.

The sense of Belonging extended to nature as well. Animals, plants, people, and streams all were interdependent. From their earliest years, children learned through stories that if this harmony was upset, tragedies could result. All are related, and one's actions impinge on the natural environment. Maintaining balanced ecological relationships is a way of ensuring balance in one's own life.[18]

Charles Eastman (his Dakota name was *Ohiyesa*) was among the first Native Americans to receive a doctor of medicine degree in 1889. After tending the survivors of the Wounded Knee massacre, he became a prolific author describing how children were reared in traditional Native culture: "The old are dedicated to the service of the young, as their teachers and advisers, and the young in turn regard them with love and reverence."[19]

Belonging to a cross-generational extended family is the normal kinship pattern of Indigenous peoples worldwide. Thus, the building block of Maori society is *whanau*, a three-generation family which ensures children have many adults to care for them, including grandparents and other elders.[20] Western colonization severely disrupted this supportive ecology.

Much as it may feel normal to anyone raised in Western traditions, the nuclear family of Western society is an oddity in the long history of human civilization. If a family is downsized to one or two biological parents, caregivers face great challenges in providing parental support and meeting growth needs.[21]

Not only does it take a village to raise a child, but it takes a village to meet each adult's emotional needs. A couple living alone in an urban apartment does not have the support of family members who may live far away. All duties of parental care fall to these adults or a single, working parent. Is it any wonder that they would feel stress in their lives that goes beyond their cognitive limits to handle? While it is not feasible to reconstruct extended family kinship systems, it is time to ask the critical question, "Who do we call family?"[22]

In the traditional extended family, many adults share the responsibility for rearing children, giving the biological parents respite in their parenting duties. Likewise, a network of family members offers mutual support so a parent can rely on more than an individual spouse. Lynda Gray describes the traditional First Nations family of Canada:

Children were considered sacred and were mentored throughout life about the traditional teachings and ways of their Nation
so that they would grow to know their responsibilities and
rights within their family and community. Parenting was not
confined to the biological parents; rather it was shared with
grandparents, siblings, aunts and uncles. Other individuals also
became involved in mentoring children.[23]

Contemporary civilization is threatened by a loss of the very sense
of community that characterizes tribal peoples. One Native person
summed it up long ago: "You are each a one-man tribe."[24] The challenge is to build relational supports that can serve as new tribes
for children and youth. The family, school, faith organization, and
community all have the potential to help fill this void.

The Spirit of Mastery

In addition to biological and interpersonal needs, children and
adults strive for mastery of their environments. Robert W. White
refers to this need as *competence motivation*.[25] When the need to
be competent is satisfied, motivation for further achievement is
enhanced; deprived of opportunities for success, young people
express their frustration through troubled behavior or by retreating
in helplessness and inferiority.

Father gave me my first pony and also my first lesson in riding.
The pony was a very gentle one and I was so small that he
tied me in place on the pony's back. In time I sat on my horse
by myself and then I rode by father's side. That was real
achievement, for I was very small indeed.

—Standing Bear[26]

Mastery is the drive to strengthen one's knowledge, skill, or talent.[27]
Research that defines *intelligence* as a person's ability to respond successfully to challenges and learn from experience has replaced earlier

views that intelligence is fixed.[28] Robert Sternberg identifies three types of intelligence: (1) *analytic intelligence* is the ability to solve problems, (2) *creative intelligence* involves new ways of doing things, and (3) *practical intelligence* is the intuitive ability to solve problems in everyday life and relationships.[29]

Gregory A. Cajete has worked to reconcile Indigenous and Western perspectives on science. Native education uses the community to develop cognitive, physical, social, and spiritual competence.[30] Children learn that wisdom comes from listening to and observing elders. Ceremonies and oral legends transmit ideals to the younger generation. Stories not only entertain but also transmit knowledge and values. Games and creative play that simulate adult responsibility develop competence.

Although Native education encourages play, it balances this with an emphasis on work as well. From the earliest years, parents have nourished responsibility:

> I was asked to do little errands and my pride in doing them developed. Mother would say, "Son, bring in some wood." I would get what I was able to carry, and if it were but one stick, Mother would in some way show her pleasure.[31]

Adults also give older children responsibility for caring for those who are younger. Ella Deloria describes a grandmother tending an infant asleep in a blanket on the ground. She had to leave, so she called her own five-year-old son from his play and instructed him:

> "Cinks, stay here until I come back and take care of him. He is your little son, so do not leave him alone." Her tone was earnest, as if in conversation with an adult. "See that he is not stepped on, he is so tiny—and scare the flies for him."[32]

Sometime later, he was still on the job. While his eyes wistfully followed his playmates nearby, he stuck to his post. He had already learned that a father does not desert his son.

Success and Mastery produce social recognition as well as inner satisfaction. Native children learn to generously acknowledge the achievements of others, but a person who receives honor must always accept it without arrogance. Those more skilled than oneself become models, not competitors:

> There was always one, or a few in every band, who swam the best, who shot the truest arrow, or who ran the fastest, and I at once set their accomplishment as the mark for me to attain. In spite of all this striving, there was no sense of rivalry. We never disliked the boy who did better than the others. On the contrary, we praised him. All through our society, the individual who excelled was praised and honored.[33]

The simple wisdom of Native culture is that, since all need to feel competent, all require encouragement in their competency. Striving is for attainment of a personal goal, not for being superior to one's opponent. Just as one feels ownership in the success of others, one also learns to share personal achievements with others. Success becomes a possession of the many, not of the privileged few.

The Spirit of Independence

Traditional Native culture placed a high value on respecting individual Autonomy and decision making. Survival outside of the camp circle depended upon making good judgments, so training in self-management began in early childhood. The emphasis on respecting the power of each person led to democratic governance systems among Native American and First Nations peoples. The founding fathers of the United States acknowledged their debt to the Iroquois Confederacy for the democratic principles that shaped the U.S. Constitution.[34]

The term *independence* can be confusing since it has a host of meanings including empowerment, freedom, assertiveness, strong-willed, self-determination, self-confidence, self-governance, and even the lack of dependence on others. The dominant cultural lens of individualism leads to the misperception that the goal of independence is *self-sufficiency*. We believe Independence is best understood as *responsibility*, which relates to ways we exercise personal power.

- *Self-control* is the first step to Independence—the power to regulate one's emotions and impulses.
- *Self-confidence* is a sense of personal power—belief in the ability to influence others and shape one's destiny.
- *Shared responsibility* involves limits on one's power— respecting the rights and autonomy of others.

Modern researchers describe a similar process for classroom teachers as the *gradual release of responsibility*.[35] With this framework, educators gradually transfer the responsibility for learning to students as they grow to become increasingly capable of managing that responsibility.

We Indians laid the foundation of freedom and equality long before any Europeans came and took it up, but they do not give us credit.

—*Charles A. Eastman*[36]

Similarly, and in contrast to obedience-focused models of discipline, Native child-rearing follows the principle of guidance without interference. Elders teach values and provide models, but the child receives increasing opportunities to learn to make choices without coercion. Standing Bear explains:

> For an elder person in the Lakota tribe to strike or punish a young person was an unthinkable brutality. Such an ugly thing as force with anger back of it was unknown to me, for it was never exhibited in my presence.[37]

The goal of external discipline is to build internal discipline. This view is grounded in a respect for the right of all persons to control their own destiny. The belief is that children respond to positive nurturance, but force cannot make them be responsible. Even when it might be easier for the adult to take over, adults are patient and allow children to solve problems in their own manner. In Edward Hoffman's biography on his life, Abraham H. Maslow described how Blackfoot children learned personal Autonomy:

> I can remember a toddler trying to open a door to a cabin. He could not make it. This was a big, heavy door, and he was shoving and shoving. Well, Americans would get up and open the door for him. The Blackfoot Indians sat for half an hour while that baby struggled with that door, until he was able to get it open himself. He had to grunt and sweat, and then everyone praised him because he was able to do it himself.[38]

Maslow concluded that Blackfoot Indians respected children more than Americans did. Throughout his life, Maslow would remain a staunch advocate of this firm yet loving approach to building confident, emotionally secure youth.

Native elders believed that if children are to be taught responsibility, they must approach children with maturity and dignity. In the 19th-century treatise on the American Indian, Elijah M. Haines observes that "they are fond of their children and treat them with the greatest respect and consideration."[39]

The main strategy of behavior control was verbal communication, which began as soon as the child could understand language. Blue Whirlwind relates, "We never struck our children for we loved them. Rather we talked to them gently, but never harshly. If they were doing something wrong, we asked them to stop."[40]

Such gentleness did not imply permissiveness. As a Native elder explains, parents set clear expectations and, if children failed to meet responsibilities, they received a thorough lecture.[41] This did not involve preaching, although the elder was in charge and the youth was listening. Instead, adults explained how others would be hurt or disappointed, or how persons who acted in cruel ways would not have friends.

Standing Bear portrays an approach to rewards and punishments that challenges many contemporary theories of child management. He does not recall his father saying, "You have to do this," but instead he would often say something like, "Son, some day when you are a man you will do this."[42]

Adults never offered children prizes or rewards for doing something well. The achievement itself was the appropriate reward and to put anything above this was to plant unhealthy ideas in the minds of children and make them weak. In place of rewards and punishments were modeling, group influence, discussion, and positive expectations—all practices that modern educators and youth practitioners can adopt.

Contemporary behavioral science is only just beginning to understand Native concepts of instilling responsibility instead of obedience. In their research on self-determination theory, Richard M. Ryan and Edward L. Deci note that *autonomy* literally means self-governing in contrast to being controlled by others.[43] This does not mean unfettered freedom, since humans must balance basic needs for relatedness and autonomy. Recall from the start of this section that true independence depends on self-control, self-confidence, and shared responsibility. Phrased in the context of Henry W. Maier's simple meme, the challenge is *to be attached and to be free*.[44] The ability of children to gain responsible self-control is related to the security of their attachments.[45]

Discipline never really succeeds if it does not recognize the universal need of all persons to be free, to be in control of themselves, and to be able to influence others. Martin L. Hoffman cites research showing that behavior management by power assertion causes children to perceive moral standards as externally imposed.[46] Many resist such control or respond only when under the threat of external sanctions. He posits that an alternative strategy is to help children understand the effect of their behavior on others while fostering empathy and responsibility.

Growth toward independence does not mean that a young person no longer has a need for nurturance. Many who work with adolescents confuse these needs by disengaging from dependency relationships while perpetuating behavioral dependence. Native childcare philosophy recognized the necessity of harmonizing apparently conflicting needs by blending Autonomy with Belonging.

The Spirit of Generosity

Generosity is more than an ethical principle; it is mapped in our genes. As psychiatrist Bruce D. Perry observes, children are born for love.[47] William Damon describes how the human brain is programmed to provide a burst of inspiration when we act with empathy and benevolence.[48] Only by being of value to others can humans derive the full satisfaction of a meaningful and purposeful life.

Children are the purpose of life. We were once children, and someone cared for us, and now it is our time to care.

—*Eddie Belleroe, Cree Elder*[49]

Children in Native cultures often sat in a circle while an older person talked to them of what was ahead as they became adults and what they should do to live good lives.[50] A recurrent message was that the highest virtue was to be generous and unselfish. Long before he could participate in the hunt, a boy would look forward to that day when he would bring home his first game and give it to persons in need.[51] These teachings form the heart of altruistic Generosity and are instilled from earliest childhood. When a mother would share food with the needy, she would give portions to her children for them to share, so they could experience the satisfaction of giving.[52]

Adults instructed children to always share generously without holding back. Eastman tells of his grandmother teaching him to give away what he cherished most so that he would become strong and courageous.[53] Giving was a part of many ceremonies, such as a marriage or a memorial to a loved one. People engaged in gift-giving upon the least provocation, children brought food to their elders' tipis, and women made useful and artistic presents for orphans and widows. Prestige was accorded to those who gave unreservedly. To accumulate property for its own sake was disgraceful.[54]

Unlike communal societies where property is owned collectively, individual ownership prevailed in most Native cultures. However, people did not acquire property for conspicuous consumption but to help others. Things were less important than people, and the test of one's good values was to be able to give anything without the pulse quickening. Those not observing these customs were suspicious characters whose values were based on selfishness.[55] While Generosity served to share wealth, giving had more than an economic rationale. Core values of sharing and community responsibility were deeply ingrained in the community. Giving was not confined to property but rather permeated all aspects of Native culture.

One does not have to live long among Native people to realize that the value of Generosity and sharing is still very much alive. A high school boy spends his last money on a bag of chips, walks into a recreation center, takes a handful for himself, and passes the bag to his peers. Another teenage boy proudly wears a new jacket to a school dance. For the next few months, the jacket makes the rounds of cousins and friends until the original owner wears it again.[56]

In this value system, one can be happy without measuring the worth of others by their possessions. Members of the dominant culture who define success in terms of personal wealth fail to recognize the power of Generosity. Yet, for millennia, this value system has made life meaningful and enabled people to overcome adversity. Giving was the delight of Native peoples: "The greatest brave was he who could part with his cherished belongings and at the same time sing songs of joy and praise."[57]

Native culture and authentic democracy share the fundamental tenet of concern for the welfare of all others in the community. There are many calls for cultivating Generosity and Altruism among contemporary youth.[58] The Search Institute documents how service-learning activities foster positive youth development. Extensive research shows long-term outcomes of reduced risks (such as substance abuse, violence, and school problems) and increased thriving (school success, civic engagement, and becoming a leader).[59] Youth increase their sense of self worth as they become committed to the positive value of caring for others.

Completing the Circle

The shape of a simple circle reflects the interrelationship of all of creation. Although the medicine wheel is identified with Native American cultures, other forms of the sacred circle are found in Indigenous cultures worldwide.[60] When the Circle of Courage is complete, humans live in harmony and balance. When it is broken, discouragement ensues.

The circle is a sacred symbol of all life.

—Virginia Driving Hawk Sneve[61]

Children show problems when needs are unmet, or they may compensate by meeting needs in distorted ways. Thus, a youth who lacks Belonging may seek out an antisocial gang. Our challenge is to read beneath these "outside kid" behaviors to understand the private logic and goals of the person.[62] For example, adults may label undesirable behavior as *aggression*, but to understand this angry person, one may need to answer such questions as the following.

- Is this revenge by a youth who feels rejection?
- Is this frustration in response to failure?
- Is this rebellion to counter powerlessness?
- Is this exploitation in pursuit of selfish goals?

Abraham Maslow observes that problem behavior results from unmet needs—and effective prevention and treatment address these needs.[63] This is a central tenet of research on resilience and positive youth development.[64]

Table 2.1 highlights examples of behavior when needs are met, when needs go unmet, and when youth pursue distorted ways to meet their needs; for example, joining a gang to belong. Each section of the table gives examples of behaviors often related to one of the four values in the Circle of Courage. Adults are more effective in dealing with challenging students when they understand how these developmental needs powerfully shape both positive and negative behavior.

When youths have unmet needs relative to the Circle of Courage, they often exhibit common behaviors.

- **Belonging needs unmet:** Some who feel rejected disengage from human attachment. Others compensate with artificial belongings such as joining a gang. These needs can be met by trusting relationships.
- **Mastery needs unmet:** Those frustrated by failure may give up in futility. Others seek competence in distorted ways, such as delinquent skills. All need opportunities for meaningful achievement.

Table 2.1: Linking Needs to Behavior

Belonging	Need Unmet	Need Distorted
Attachment	Disconnection	Attention seeking
Trust	Distrust	Hypervigilance
Cooperation	Isolation	Gang affiliation
Mastery	**Need Unmet**	**Need Distorted**
Achievement	Failure	Delinquent skills
Problem solving	Give up easily	Manipulative
Motivation	Unmotivated	Overly competitive
Independence	**Need Unmet**	**Need Distorted**
Autonomy	Helplessness	Oppositional
Self-control	Impulsivity	Over-controlling
Assertiveness	Easily misled	Intimidating
Generosity	**Need Unmet**	**Need Distorted**
Altruism	Selfishness	Used by others
Caring	Lack of empathy	Overly indulgent
Contributing	Lack of purpose	Hedonistic

- **Independence needs unmet:** Lacking power, some feel helpless. Others compensate with rebellion or defiance. All need to develop self-control and self-confidence, using power in prosocial ways.

- **Generosity needs unmet:** Those without empathy for others may lack purpose in life. Some seek to compensate in hedonistic pleasure seeking. The antidote is altruism, being of value to others.

When needs are fulfilled, people attain what psychiatrist Karl Menninger calls "the vital balance."[65] The circle is complete.

As anthropologist John Collier observes, Natives Americans have survived centuries of attempts at annihilation. Living in harmony with all of nature is their enduring vision: "Could we make it our own, there would be an internally inexhaustible earth and a forever lasting peace."[66]

We conclude this chapter with the descriptors for the four Circle of Courage principles listed in table 2.2. These practical examples of developmental relationships are markers of resilience.

Table 2.2: The Circle of Courage Supports and Strengths

Belonging	Mastery
• I am close to my parent or caregiver. • There are other adults in my life I trust. • My teachers really care about students. • I have a friend who knows me well. • I am accepted in a group of my peers.	• I usually pay attention in school. • I feel I am making progress in school. • My family encourages my school success. • Teachers expect me to try hard and succeed. • My friends want me to do my best in school.
Independence	**Generosity**
• I can keep calm in stressful situations. • I think for myself and take responsibility. • I keep trying even when things get difficult. • I don't act superior but show others respect. • I usually get along with those in authority.	• It bothers me if people are mean to others. • When someone is upset, I try to help him or her. • My family supports one another in hard times. • My friends help and encourage one another. • I find purpose in life by contributing to others.

CHAPTER 3

Seeds of
Discouragement

*Life itself is the greatest teacher, and each person
must accept the hard realities of life along with
those that are joyous and pleasing.*

—*Gregory A. Cajete*[1]

Simply stated, when youth at risk are discouraged, then the Circle
of Courage is broken. In essence, *discouragement* is the absence of
courage. Preeminent psychologist Alfred Adler used these terms
in the early 20th century to describe what we call *risk* and *resilience*.[2] Through this lens, courage is something both Western and
Indigenous cultures see as a key virtue.[3]

In an intensive study of Canadian programs for youth at risk, James P.
Anglin concludes that all of them "experienced deep and pervasive
psycho-emotional pain."[4] Anglin coined the term *pain-based behavior*
to describe acting out or withdrawal reactions, which are a residue
of unresolved past trauma. Yet, few who worked with these youths
had the training necessary to recognize or address the pain that self-
defeating or acting-out behavior masks. Instead, the typical intervention included a sharp verbal reprimand or threat of consequences.

If we focus on defiant or destructive behavior, the young person
becomes the problem. As Nicholas Hobbs observes, when children
disturb or disrupt us, we label *them* as disturbed or disruptive.[5]

By seeing the problem behavior as tied to pain, we are motivated to respond to needs.

Once we understand the inner world of a youth in distress, a very different picture emerges. Attuned to the person's pain, we shift from blame to empathy. Instead of asking "What is wrong with you?" the question becomes "What has happened to you?" From the resilience perspective, "What is *strong* with you?"

Cultures exist to meet human needs. But there is growing evidence that modern culture is mismatched to how humans are biologically designed to live. The result is a breakdown in health, emotional well-being, and social harmony.[6] We cannot alter our genes, but we can change our environments.

Native American educators Adrienne Brant James (Mohawk) and Tammy Lunday (Dakota) contrast two systems for governing human societies—(1) cultures of respect and (2) cultures of dominance.[7] Table 3.1 shows these systems.

Table 3.1: A Contrast of Cultures

Cultures of Respect	Cultures of Dominance
Belonging Have trusting bonds in a community of mutual support	**Alienation** Display disconnection from family, school, and community
Mastery Show motivation to learn in order to develop competence	**Superiority** Show motivation to win to appear better than others
Independence Recognize all persons' right for autonomy	**Intimidation** Use power to rank and subjugate others
Generosity Show empathy and concern for others	**Privilege** Pursues the "good life" in self-centered materialism

When we meet children's needs through respectful relationships, children thrive. But as Urie Bronfenbrenner observes, there is widespread alienation in the ecology of family, school, peers, and community.[8] Children and adolescents who experience repeated stress without relational support display a host of emotional, behavioral, and learning problems.[9]

Disconnected from family, friends, school, or community, the seeds of discouragement are sown in the world of childhood. We show these *circles of influence* in figure 3.1.[10] In every area of the ecology, needs are either met or neglected. When children show serious behavior problems, this is usually a symptom of *dis-ease* in the ecology rather than *disease* in the child. Every area of the ecology can either foster growth or fuel problems.

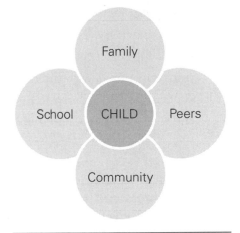

Figure 3.1: The ecology of childhood.

Disconnected youth receive a multitude of labels, most of them unfriendly. They are described as aggressive or anxious, as attention-disordered or antisocial, as unmotivated or unteachable, as addicts or dropouts. Most terms are either overtly hostile or subtly patronizing. All such terms are condescending.

Adopting a strength-based philosophy shifts the focus from labeling liabilities to building assets. In this chapter, we address four ecological hazards in the lives of youth at risk.

1. **Relational trauma:** Youth who have suffered conflict, terror, and loss, and who expect to be hurt again

2. **Failure as futility:** Youth who are insecure and feel crippled by feelings of inadequacy and incompetence

3. **Powerlessness:** Youth whose lack of control over their lives leads to helplessness, impulsiveness, or rebellion

4. **Loss of purpose:** Youth who are searching for meaning in a world of confusing values

Relational Trauma

Children whose basic needs are unmet learn that adults are unreliable. Some reach beyond their families in search of substitute belongings with other adults or peers. Others become *relationship-wary*, viewing even friendly, helpful adults with deep distrust. Expecting rejection, they employ protective behaviors learned in prior encounters with threatening persons.[11] The following story of Richard Cardinal shows the depth of relationship hunger in such a child, and the tragic failure to reclaim this alienated youth.

If you feel safe and loved, your brain becomes specialized in exploration, play, and cooperation. If you are frightened and unwanted, it specializes in managing feelings of fear and abandonment.

—*Bessel van der Kolk*[12]

The Psychological Orphan

Richard Cardinal was born into a Canadian Métis community, people of mixed First Nations and European ancestors. He and his siblings were removed from alcoholic parents and dispersed to foster care, generally with white families. Richard spent thirteen years being shunted to a string of foster homes, schools, youth shelters, and treatment facilities.

An intelligent, thoughtful youth, Richard withdrew into himself and began expressing his loneliness in a diary. Teachers were not successful in reaching out to him or cultivating his talent. He described himself as an outcast, and his pain broke through in acts of desperation. He ran away, heading for the North like a salmon swimming upstream to its place of origin. He stole a car, shot a cow, and made several attempts at suicide, the first time in school. Once he was found sitting in front of a 7-Eleven store bleeding from the wrists. Another time, he was curled in a doghouse with *please help me* written in his own blood. Finally, cut off from human bonds, failing in school, powerless to control his life, drowning in feelings of worthlessness, Richard Cardinal, age seventeen, hanged himself from a board suspended between two birch trees at his last foster home.

Richard would have been just another marginalized person whose death attracted no more attention than his life but for a powerful documentary produced by the National Film Board of Canada.[13] The First Nations director Alanis Obomsawin captured the attention of a nation that failed to give this boy what he desperately needed. These excerpts from Richard Cardinal's diary, as narrated in the documentary, reveal the depth of loneliness in this sensitive youth:

> I had four hours before I would leave my family and friends behind. I went into the bedroom and dug out my old harmonica. I went down to the barnyard and sat on the fence. I began to play real slow and sad-like for the occasion, but halfway through the song, my lower lip began to quiver, and I knew I was going to cry. And I was glad, so I didn't even try to stop myself. I guess that my foster mother heard me and must have come down to comfort me. When she put her arm around me, I pulled away and ran up the roadway.

> I didn't want no one to love any more. I had been hurt too many times. So I began to learn the art of blocking out all emotions and shut out the rest of the world. The door would open to no one.

> I'm skipping the rest of the years because it continues to be the same. I want to say to people involved in my life, don't take this personally. I just can't take it anymore.

> Love can be gentle as a lamb or ferocious as a lion. It is something to be welcomed and to be afraid of. It is good and bad, yet

people live, fight, die for this. Somehow people can cope with it. I don't know. I think I would not be happy with it, yet I am depressed and sad without it. Love is very strange.

The Hunger for Belonging

Contemporary society is creating a growing number of children at risk for relational trauma. The decline of extended families and intimate neighborhoods leaves an isolated nuclear family. While the family is crucial in socializing children, Indigenous cultures are not limited to biological parents since the tribe nourishes the new generation.[14]

Stabilizing and strengthening families are high priorities.[15] But there will always be children born to adults whose parenting skills and resources are insufficient to meet their needs. All sectors of the community have resources to bring to this problem. Whether educators and other youth practitioners are ready for this responsibility or not, they have a key role in reclaiming children adrift.

Building restorative relationships is not limited to those with formal training in counseling. An adult who is involved in ongoing daily events has many opportunities to show small acts of kindness and respect. While trained therapists make important contributions, everyday supportive relationships are the most potent way to heal trauma. Clinical psychologist Ricky Greenwald writes:

> You do not have to be a therapist to create a therapeutic or healing relationship with a child. Parents, counselors, teachers, coaches, direct care workers, case managers, and others are all in a position to help a child heal. The quality of your relationship is the vehicle for healing.[16]

In every city and hamlet, schools could become the new *tribes* to support and nurture children and adolescents at risk.[17] The school is the only institution providing ongoing, long-term relationships with *all* our young. Some children spend only minutes a day in conversation with parents, but all have extended contact with adults who staff our schools. Unless all educators rise to such challenges, schools further alienation.

The structure of large traditional schools can impede such interpersonal relationships. Students and teachers do not relate to one another as whole persons but in narrow circumscribed roles. Communication is restricted to what one can and must do in a fifty-minute period dominated by teacher-directed behavior. Often, the only spontaneity is disruptive behavior which divides students and teachers into adversarial camps. At each higher level of education, relationships increasingly lack meaning and personal satisfaction. Students at greatest risk of dropping out are those not connected with any teacher.[18]

Without stable adults, socialization is left to peers and child-parents. Hungry for fun and friendship, these children roam the halls of schools and the streets of cities in pursuit of meaningful relationships, often with other disconnected youth.

Even when families lack stability, the most formidable influence on the development of children continues to be parents. Thus, education and child welfare policies mandate parental partnership.[19] Yet, professionals skillful at connecting with difficult youth are less comfortable working with parents.

Professionals and parents time-share responsibility for youth, but genuine partnerships are rare. Mutual blaming contests are not. Research shows that parents lodge responsibility first with the school, second with the child, and third with themselves. In contrast, school personnel blame problems first on the home, then on the child, and last on the school.[20] Such displacement of problem ownership fails to identify problems and solutions. Subsequent chapters will explore successful reclaiming strategies which involve collaboration of all stakeholders.

Failure as Futility

Early pioneers in work with difficult youth were incurable optimists who could always find cause for hope in the face of the most difficult problems. At the dawn the 19th century, Swiss educator Johann H. Pestalozzi created a castle school for outcast street children to demonstrate his revolutionary thesis that "precious hidden faculties" could be found beneath an appearance of ignorance.[21] In that same era, physician Jean Marc Itard shocked the intellectuals of Paris by declaring that he could educate a wolf-child in *The Wild Boy of Aveyron.*[22]

Every great cause is born from repeated failures and from imperfect achievements.

—Maria Montessori[23]

In the 20th century, Maria Montessori advocated new approaches to disadvantaged children who had absorbent minds but were pinned like mounted butterflies to their desks.[24] In the same vein, Sylvia Ashton-Warner of New Zealand castigated the lock-step colonial education that enslaved intelligent, resourceful Maori children in roles of powerless inferiority.[25]

In contrast to these hopeful pioneers, pessimism is common in contemporary approaches to difficult youth. Negative environments and expectations can produce failure and futility in young people as well as the adults who share their lives. Both practice wisdom and scientific research identify the following factors that impede learning and achievement.

- **Negative expectations:** Johann H. Pestalozzi created schools for street kids after the French revolution, believing that love and learning would unleash their positive potentials. A mass of research on the *Pygmalion effect* shows that it is accurate——expectations can breed hope or futility in both students and staff.[26]

- **Punishment:** In the 19th century, Horace Mann advised teachers to treat difficult students like physicians who find challenge in solving hard cases. Punishing a struggling learner is as illogical as a surgeon attacking the limb he is treating. Yet punishment persists despite discredited zero-tolerance policies.[27]

- **Boredom:** In the 20th century, Jane Addams saw how a lack of adventure plagued urban youth.[28] She detailed how, when the United States was a coastal nation, rowdy boys were sent to sea and would return months later as men and concluded that 20th century youth were instead finding thrills in delinquent behavior. She called for tapping the spirit of youth, and in the 21st century, there is renewed interest in enhancing achievement and student well-being by instilling joy in learning.[29]

- **Purposelessness:** At the dawn of the 20th century, G. Stanley Hall wrote of the powerful idealism of adolescence;[30] and William James proposed harnessing this spirit of service to society as "the moral equivalent of war."[31] But only a fifth of modern youth are thriving. Young people need to be engaged in some great cause that gives purpose to their lives.[32]

Folk Psychology

Most of our everyday responses to others are not a result of formal training but rather *folk psychology*. Also known as *commonsense psychology*, this is our human capacity to explain and predict the behavior and thinking of other people. Folk psychology is a result of life experiences as well as the design of the human brain.[33]

When we try to make sense of another person's behavior, we attribute traits and motivation to him or her. Thus, we intuitively make assumptions about the characteristics of the other person and his or her intentions. If someone causes us distress, we are primed to label the person in negative terms and to see problems as intentional. Those who look for positive traits in the person and interpret behavior with empathy are better able to disengage from knee-jerk negativism.[34]

When under stress, humans have a strong tendency to revert to negative theories to interpret behavior. One of the most common distortions in folk psychology is called the *fundamental attribution error*.[35] We use a double standard in judging others and ourselves. Thus, we view aggression of others as a flaw in their character, but our own angry behavior is justified.

In most disciplines, the expert thinks differently than the novice. But whatever their training, many dealing with difficult children are locked in pessimistic folk psychology. They react to the behavior of the outside child rather than responding to the needs of the inside child.[36] Psychology and poverty expert Erik K. Laursen observes, "When youth practitioners ignore the inside kid and attempt to change young people from the outside, they do not support the development of resilience."[37]

Table 3.2 shows how negative folk psychology theories can shape attitudes and behaviors—even among those embracing professional theories. When we feel angry or threatened, our brains unconsciously switch into fight-or-flight mode. As Nicholas J. Long, Mary M. Wood, and Frank A. Fecser have shown, those working with challenging youth need specific training in disengaging from conflict cycles.[38]

A robust positive psychology movement is challenging deficit perspectives.[39] But pessimism still pervades professional theories of behavior. A lingering vestige of the deficit mindset is the *Diagnostic and Statistical Manual of Mental Disorders (DSM-5)* of the American Psychiatric Association (APA).[40] This ever-expanding tome turns adjustment problems into "disorders" for children and adolescents. Consider the following.

- Childhood psychopathy has become a category of Conduct Disorder, but most teens given this diagnosis do not show such problems as adults.[41]

- Children with temper tantrums often receive the ominous sounding diagnosis of Disruptive Mood Disorder, which is a boon for Big Pharma.[42]

- Diagnostic labels mask trauma; when defined as a disorder, the prevailing intervention is to prescribe drugs rather than therapy.[43]

Table 3.2: Folk Psychology in Theories About Difficult Youth

Orientation	Problem	Deficit-Based Reactions
Intuition	Deviance	Criticize, attack, ostracize
Folk religion	Demons	Chastise, exorcise, banish
Biophysical	Disease	Diagnose, drug, hospitalize
Behavioral	Disorder	Assess, control, coerce
Correctional	Delinquency	Adjudicate, punish, imprison
Social work	Dysfunction	Intake, manage, discharge
Educational	Disobedience	Reprimand, suspend, expel
Special education	Disability	Label, remediate, segregate

Abraham Maslow describes how we interpret the problem behavior based on our own generalized optimism or pessimism, and assuming the worst is a dominant tendency.[44] A common practice in psychology and education is to use behavior checklists to assess challenging children. Many such instruments list problems but they ignore potentials.

Figure 3.2 (page 42) contrasts strength and deficit perspectives of troubled children. A century ago in a spirit of optimism, Karl Wilker reformed youth justice in Germany with a focus on the former. The deficit description is from a widely used textbook on exceptional children. Some might argue that this is just idealism versus reality, but these are profoundly different mindsets.

The Strength Perspective	The Deficit Perspective
"We want to find and strengthen the healthy elements in young people, no matter how deeply they are hidden. We enthusiastically believe in the existence of those qualities even in the seemingly worst of our adolescents."	*"They are abusive, destructive, unpredictable, irresponsible, bossy, quarrelsome, irritable, jealous, defiant—anything but pleasant to be with. Naturally adults choose not to spend time with this kind of child."*
—Karl Wilker describing his work in a Berlin youth prison in 1921[45]	—A 21st century text on children with emotional and behavioral disorders[46]

Figure 3.2: Contrasting strength and deficit perspectives.

Certainly, one cannot communicate without using some negative labels. However, a goal in building resilience is to discover the potential greatness in every individual. The German poet and educator Johann Wolfgang von Goethe observes that almost every fault is but a hard shell enclosing the germ of virtue.[47] When we recast *stubbornness* as *persistence*, then a liability becomes a potential asset.

Powerlessness

Early educational pioneers saw schools as laboratories in democracy where students could practice responsible citizenship.[48] Yet a common well-meaning statement is that youth are our *future* citizens, which implies they are not yet ready to exercise power. Anthropologist Ruth Benedict criticized American culture for excluding youth from responsibility only to blame them for their irresponsibility.[49] Those not secure in their personal power show various problems.

- *Helplessness* from feeling like pawns of others
- *Rebellion* by struggling to break the chains of authority
- *Narcissism* in a society devoid of social responsibility
- *Abuse of power* by intimidating or exploiting others

In his education treatise, *Emile*, Jean-Jacques Rousseau describes how adults perpetuate irresponsibility. Obedience training makes children machines in the hands of others. Punishment motivates children to deceive authority. Indulging selfish children makes them think they own the universe. Adult influence pales compared to the power of peers: "The lessons pupils get from one another in the schoolyard are a hundred times more useful than everything they will ever be told in class."[50]

Responsibility is the first step in responsibility.
                                        —W. E. B. Du Bois[51]

Neither permissive nor authoritarian approaches can reclaim young people who embrace lifestyles of freedom without responsibility. Youth see adults who place no demands on them as impotent, but to demand submission from them is to fuel rebellion and the rejection of adult values. The formidable challenge is to develop new approaches that avoid the pitfalls of either adult weakness or authoritarian obedience.

Indulgence and Irresponsibility

Rousseau observes that giving a child whatever he or she desires teaches him or her to regard others as his or her slaves.[52] Adults must distinguish between a child's needs and wants. While we should richly nourish needs, to cater to every whim is a blueprint for creating a young tyrant.

The failure to set limits erodes self-worth because children are unsure of what behaviors will gain approval.[53] Sometimes what looks like permissiveness is best described as parental neglect which fuels feelings of worthlessness.[54] Dan Olweus shows that parental tolerance for aggression is also a precursor for peer mistreatment.[55] Programs to prevent school bullying have only been marginally successful because they often fail to instill values of respect.[56]

Democratic child-rearing techniques foster responsibility and moral development; without a reasonable amount of freedom, a child cannot develop autonomy.[57] Still, whether in family, school, or community, children need adults who provide both love and limits—setting behavior standards and meeting developmental needs.[58]

Adults overwhelmed by their own problems have difficulty rearing children. This is common among single mothers struggling with poverty. Also, many teen parents lack the maturity and skills for positive parenting. The result is *neglect*, which can cause a youth to feel unloved and worthless. John R. Seita describes what these children are missing: "Parents who provide consistent affection, emotional and physical safety, boundaries, limits and expectations, opportunities, role modeling, belonging, unconditional love, and spiritual values foster the healthy development of Family Privilege."[59]

Neglect strips the child of family privilege and interferes with all these needs. Those who mentor can help provide the supports these young people desperately need.

Loss of Purpose

From the dawn of human history, people have bonded together for mutual protection and support. However difficult existence may have been, the goal of life was to ensure the survival of oneself *and* the tribe. Neurologist and psychologist Viktor E. Frankl notes that, in modern times, the struggle for survival has subsided. The new question becomes, *Survival for what?*[60] Many have the means to live but no meaning to their existence.

We have placed far too much emphasis on superficial and transitory markers of success rather than on enduring, life fulfilling goals.

—William Damon[61]

Young people cannot develop a sense of their own value unless they have opportunities to be of value to others. Ralph Waldo Emerson observes that "it is one of the most beautiful compensations of this life that no man can sincerely help another without helping himself."[62] But in contemporary society, this spirit of mutual caring is often lost in the selfish pursuit of individual goals. The Jeffersonian concept of "life, liberty and the pursuit of happiness"[63] has mutated to a life free of social responsibility in the pursuit of personal gain.

The Erosion of Community

Organizational development expert Peter Block contends that we are living in an age of isolation.[64] The dominant narrative is fear, being unsafe in our homes and communities and threatened by others unlike ourselves. Universal values of hospitality, generosity, and welcoming strangers are lost in the quest to gain or even just maintain power and personal privilege.

Robert D. Putnam documents the loss of community in his best-selling book *Bowling Alone*.[65] He finds that health, educational achievement, and economic vitality are all related to the quality of relationships in the community. Geography, financial wealth, or cultural heritage do not determine whether a town thrives. Rather, it is the quality of relationships among citizens, which is called *social capital*.

The essential challenge is to transform the isolation and self-interest within our communities into connectedness and caring for the whole.

—Peter Block[66]

Transforming communities will not come top-down from corporate or political leaders. Instead, a shift in the thinking of individual citizens is more vital than a shift in the thinking of our formal leaders. Block proposes that if we want to change the community, all we need is to change the conversation. The shift is from problems, fear, and retribution to possibility, generosity, and restoration.

Media shapes the common conversation, and the lead story in every newscast tends to be about crime and human conflict. Yet the media is not the problem for it reflects our citizenry. Powerful forces market fear for profit and politics. Fear drives our priorities, policies, and legislation. We lock down schools, put people with problems in prisons, consume mind-altering drugs, and reduce tolerance to zero.

"Restoration is about healing our fragmentation and incivility."[67] We move from depending on our leaders to having faith in our neighbors. Our differences are not problems but a source of vitality. We become *citizens*, willingly committed to the well-being of the whole.

Belonging in a small group is the core of community—we change the world one classroom, family, or peer group at a time. But this is not ingroup isolation; we extend hospitality to persons who are not used to being together, or even belonging at all. Even if they say *no* at first, we let them know they will always be welcome in the future. Communities are built as we gather together in circles.

The huge expansion of social media reflects the unmet hunger for genuine human connection. In her book *Alone Together*, Sherry Turkle contends that the very internet that brings us together can keep us apart.[68] Her fascinating interviews are with young people who are digital natives, who have grown up with online robotic connections which too often substitute for genuine human connections. She concludes that, as a result, we expect more from technology and less from one another.

Amplifying this theme in *Humans Are Underrated*, Geoff Colvin contends that technology distracts us from the powerful reality that humans are hardwired for human interaction.[69] It is in our brain-based nature to value companionship, concern for others, and acting in groups. Social relationships are the reason for our mental life and, without these alliances, we die. Therefore, our education and youth development should focus on strengthening these most essential human abilities—empathy, creativity, social sensitivity, storytelling, humor, and relationships. These, not the artificial logic of machines, will be the high-value skills of the future.

Finally, in their book *The Spirit Level*, Richard Wilkinson and Kate Pickett assemble a mass of evidence of how greater equality and sense of community makes society stronger.[70] Taking the long view, there has been an almost unstoppable historic trend toward egalitarian societies. Yet, there are dramatic reversals where a profound disparity of wealth upends this progress. Specifically, a nation's gap between the richest and poorest is the most powerful measure of health in a society.

When the privileged hoard resources, empathy for those in need erodes and the anger of those less fortunate erupts. Trust in the community is directly related to hard statistics on health, life expectancy, education, mental health, and crime. Everything comes undone in a culture of greed.

The Misery of Unimportance

Kurt Hahn, who headed schools in Germany and Great Britain, described modern youth as suffering from the "misery of unimportance."[71] In earlier times, youth were indispensable for the survival of the family and community. Working in the fields and shops beside their elders, they built a life and a nation. Extended families and cohesive neighborhoods made cooperation an everyday occurrence. The young and the elderly helped one another, and large families offered abundant opportunities to give and receive love.

In modern times, all of this sounds like fantasy island. Relatives live far away and connect only through social media. Our homes are fitted with security devices, and our yards are cordoned off with fences to protect ourselves from our neighbors. An urban school secures funds for a concrete wall around its playground to protect children from stray bullets fired by warring gangs in the housing project across the street. Nobody mentions that most occupants of the project are also children, since they are on the other side of the wall.

While youth hunger for a feeling of importance, adults infantilize them. We ask little of young people except that they be consumers. A vast industry serves youth with schooling, entertainment, and goods of all kinds, but there are limited opportunities for the young themselves to contribute to the community. Various commissions periodically recommend that young people become involved in community service activities.[72] This is a promising idea, but it raises the question of the amount of time youth are presently allocating for volunteer work. Search Institute researchers find that three-quarters of young teens spent less than two hours helping others in the month prior to the survey, and one-third said they had done nothing at all.[73]

Deprived of opportunities for genuine productivity, lured into consumptive roles, young people come to believe that their lives make little difference to the world. Those who feel the most powerless develop distorted ways of thinking, which psychologists label as "external locus of control."[74] They feel like helpless pawns following somebody else's script, rather than authors who can write the drama of their own destiny. They believe they are victims of fate or the whims of powerful others.

The most striking proof of the child's unimportance is the shrinking amount of attention from adults who offer the constant refrain of not having time. Steve Charleston, Native American elder and author, describes this tyranny of time in Western culture.[75] People generally believe time is real, which of course it is not. Only recently have humans tried to organize their life around numbers on a tiny device. Real time is the cycle of the day and seasons. But we invent idioms to describe something that doesn't exist: we make time, save time, spend time, waste time, borrow time, budget time, invest time, and manage time until, in exhaustion, we call time-out.

Charleston contends that in contrast to time, relationships are real. Family, friendship, community—these are the bonds of reality that Western time is tearing apart. We invoke another *time word* to mask the continued destruction of love in our society—*quality* time. Now not only are we quantifying time, but we are qualifying it. Segmented into seconds and minutes, we try to create warm human relationships in the microwave of quick encounters.

We cannot care for children in convenient time; we cannot learn from our elders in convenient time; we cannot maintain marriages in convenient time. The result of adjusting our lives to the fiction of time inevitably leads to empty adults, lonely elders, and neglected children.

The Depersonalization of Education

A growing body of research shows that a climate of trust is a crucial factor in how well schools meet the needs of students.[76] But many forces have served to depersonalize schools. Starting in the 19th century, schools began borrowing principles from business and industry. Taylor's assembly line theory of scientific management intrigued educators. The headmaster was retitled as *superintendent* and established systems of command and control. Teachers became specialized in a factory-like labor force. The size of schools swelled in the quest for the fictional economy of scale. Formal rules and procedures replaced informal cooperative teamwork. In his 1875 book on school management, William H. Payne proclaims, "The work of teaching thus follows the law of all well-regulated industries."[77]

Schools and social service organizations continued to use corporate and military models of management. Then, a new wave crashed on corporate America. Research from business pointed to the importance of positive organizational cultures. It highlights how

a successful school, like a successful business, is a cohesive community of shared values, beliefs, rituals, and ceremonies. Human bonds
unleash a synergy of shared responsibility. All members participate
as the adversarial mentality is supplanted by a spirit of cooperation
and mutual commitment.

This science of organizational behavior is pushing schools toward
progressive theories of management.[78] Effective programs have a positive culture with shared vision and values. Yet many attempts at
reform in this direction fail because schools adopt isolated practices:
"A dab of curriculum alignment there, a tiny piece of teacher professional development over there."[79] This trivial pursuit loses sight of
what matters most.

Participants in a reclaiming organization embrace a unifying
theme of meeting the needs of those being served.[80] When schools
have a clear value system, all other relationships become consistent
with these shared values. This also is a core principle of resilience
science, creating environments where young people can heal their
discouragement, grow, and thrive.

The following chapters explore principles and practices for reclaiming youth of discouragement.

- Chapter 4, "Bonds of Trust: Strengthening Attachment,"
  examines strategies for establishing positive relationships
  with those whose lives have been marked by alienation
  (Belonging and Attachment).

- Chapter 5, "Brain-Friendly Learning: Strengthening
  Achievement," presents alternative methods for solving
  problems and building strengths to reverse failure and
  futility (Mastery and Achievement).

- Chapter 6, "Pathways to Responsibility: Strengthening
  Autonomy," highlights strategies to strengthen self-control,

self-confidence, and respect for the rights of others
(Independence and Autonomy).

- Chapter 7, "Lives With Purpose: Strengthening
  Altruism," explores ways to foster prosocial values and
  behavior in young people whose lives lack meaning
  (Generosity and Altruism).

Reclaiming requires moving beyond problems to focus on strengths
and needs.

CHAPTER 4

Bonds of Trust: Strengthening Attachment

Every child needs at least one adult who is
irrationally crazy about him or her

— *Urie Bronfenbrenner*[1]

The need for trusting relationships is as basic as hunger or thirst. Roy Baumeister gathered an impressive array of evidence showing humans have a universal biosocial need to belong.[2] There is a clear distinction between *needs* and *wants*. Unsatisfied wants may cause temporary distress, but frustrated needs inflict destructive consequences. Needs are specifically defined as "nutriments that are essential for growth, integrity, and well-being,"[3] and Belonging occupies a prominent place on the Circle of Courage because it is a need.

The great blind spot in many programs serving youth is the failure to focus like a laser on basics, and the most basic need of children is to trust. Practice-based research shows that effective teachers are those who can develop both trust and talent in previously disengaged students.[4]

Build trust!
Build talent!

53

Research also shows great differences in effectiveness of individual teachers, but levels of education or experience did not predict success.[5] Instead, a single factor—*relational trust*—separated failing from flourishing schools. This includes *teacher-student trust* as well as *teacher-parent trust, teacher-principal trust,* and *teacher-teacher trust.* Surprisingly, the research is silent about peers, *student-student trust.*

Attachment theory, pioneered by John Bowlby and Mary Ainsworth, is "the most visible and empirically grounded conceptual framework" for human development.[6] This vibrant field is the prototype of consilience, integrating developmental, cognitive, social, and personality psychology with biological science including genetics.[7]

The first signs of human attachment appear in the bonds of a child with primary caretakers. An infant does not have to learn that attraction is innate. As a child's social world expands, attachments broaden to include close relationships with other adults and friends.

An early example of attachment behavior is seen in a young child who is separated from a parent in a strange situation. Normally the child shows marked distress and tries to re-establish closeness, such as by physical contact. Children of neglectful or abusive parents learn they cannot rely on adults to meet their needs for attachment. They have insecure attachments and are torn between the desire for close contact with the adult and contrary feelings of anger or anxiety.[8] Children need warm, consistent, and stable relationships to overcome insecurity.

Children with insecure attachments do not quickly give up on unreliable adults. What people once called attention-seeking behavior is better understood as attachment behavior, namely the persistent effort to reach out and establish a secure relationship with others. Whereas experts once instructed adults to ignore attention-seeking behavior, such advice contradicts developmental research. Previous fears of spoiling children with nurturance may not be justified. In fact, the absence of secure dependence creates havoc in a child's development.

Although love-withdrawal may yield short-term control, it puts relationships at risk. Kris Juul, pioneer researcher on behavior disorders, contends that two contrasting theories divide psychology: *Must one behave in order to be loved, or be loved in order to behave?* Modern research on moral development bears out the latter.[10]

The most potent behavioral influence that an adult can have in the life of a child comes when forming an attachment. Educator and author Janusz Korczak told his staff that their authority was based on their status as beloved and admired adults.[11] But it is a major challenge to build positive bonds with children and youth who distrust adults.

Adult-Wary Children

Paul Hernandez is a resilience author and former youth at risk who grew up in an impoverished gang culture in California. He recalls that rather than trying to connect with him and his friends, "teachers and administrators simply punished us and considered us a burden in the classroom."[12] He viewed school as a hostile environment rather than a source of support to better his life. Once children and adults become enemies, a battle ensues. Hernandez describes a middle school experience:

> I specifically remember a teacher who told me one day that whenever I showed up in her class, I ruined her day. . . . It was at that moment that I decided to resist every single thing she would attempt with me to make her feel the disrespect she made me feel.[13]

Fortunately, Hernandez was ultimately able to connect with a teacher who drew out his hidden talent, and he now teaches relationship-building skills to other professionals.

The students who need us the most push us away the most.

—*Paul Hernandez*[14]

Many who work with youth at risk are motivated to enter this field because of their own personal background of relational trauma.[15] Psychiatrist Francine Cournos tragically lost both parents only to have her relatives reject her.[16] She tells the story of her transformation from the troubled girl nobody wanted and the strength that led to her becoming a doctor. In her journey through the foster care system, she hungered for love but pushed helpers away for fear of being hurt again. Here she describes her encounter with a warm young social worker:

> I liked her, I was lonely, and I longed for someone to show an interest in what was happening to me. But I couldn't allow it. . . . I started to feel fond of her, but I refused to show it. I sat in silent protest, resisting all overtures, no matter how tempting, thirsty at sea and only salt water everywhere.[17]

Another noted author on youth at risk is John R. Seita of Michigan State University who was removed from fifteen court placements by age twelve. In *Kids Who Outwit Adults*, he describes problem behavior as strategies adult-wary youth use to cope with authority figures they distrust.[18] He observes the following patterns.

- **Fight:** Some act out, displaying defiance, antagonism, and rule-breaking behavior.
- **Flight:** Others become guarded, withdrawn, and isolated or retreat into drug use.
- **Fool:** These youth mask their real feelings by manipulating, provoking, and outsmarting authority figures.
- **Follow:** Disconnected from adults, they seek out like-minded peers for substitute belonging.

The challenge for the helper is to avoid being drawn into tit-for-tat hostility and spot the unmet need beneath the behavior.

Bids for Connection

Generations of professionals were taught to ignore undesired attention-seeking behavior, and parents were advised to do the same. It is now clear that such actions are attempts to gain recognition—or in the words of Daniel, "noticement."

All I want is some kind of noticement.

—Daniel, age fifteen

Relationship science shows that humans make frequent *bids for connection.*[19] Bids might come in the form of conversation, requests for help, and even obnoxious or roughhousing behavior. Bids also can be nonverbal, like facial expressions, touch, and physical appearance (grooming and clothing, for example). Humor can also serve as a bid for connection.[20] Even when an adult makes a good-faith, positive bid to connect, a distrustful youth is likely to ignore or misinterpret the gesture.

The bid is a basic unit of emotional communication. A person receiving a bid for connection has three options.[21]

1. **Turning toward:** Reacting in positive ways to a bid

2. **Turning away:** Ignoring a bid or acting preoccupied

3. **Turning against:** Being belligerent or argumentative

John M. Gottman views emotional intelligence as the ability to bid and to respond to another's bids. Many factors affect the ability to bid, including extroverted or shy temperament. But like any other skill, children can learn to connect.

Both *turning away* and *turning against* are rejections of the bid to connect. However, *turning toward* sends the following positive messages.

- "I am interested in you."
- "I want to understand you."
- "I'd like to help you."
- "I accept you—even if not all your behavior."

Adults build positive bonds by being responsive to the bids of children. Although it is difficult to keep making positive bids to youth who may not respond in kind, these are the emotional messages they need. In *Building Bridges*, Don Parker writes on the challenges and importance of building positive, trusting teacher-student relationships.[22]

Trust-Building Strategies

Human relationships heal troubled and traumatized lives. This was a dominant ethos of the early writings in education and youth work. But as professional literature became more technical, relationships were increasingly ignored. Now there is a burgeoning science of human attachment.[23]

The quality of human relationships is more influential than the specific techniques we employ. In the words of Bill Milliken, "Programs don't change kids—relationships do."[24] Teachers with divergent instructional styles can be successful if they develop a positive classroom climate. Counselors trained in different methods succeed or fail to a large extent based on the quality of rapport with clients. Behavior management systems backfire if authority figures cannot build respectful relationships. Educator Eric Jensen, who grew up as a youth at risk, writes extensively on the need for educators to adopt both a relational mindset and a rich classroom climate when attempting to connect with youth at risk.[25]

While most recognize the importance of relationships, some are locked in narrow professional roles that insulate them from close connections with students or clients. Those who keep aloof from difficult youth often believe that distance is necessary to maintain authority and respect. Others want to help but lack skills to relate to reluctant youth.

Trust is the glue that holds teaching and learning together.
                                             —*Nicholas Hobbs*[26]

There is a solid base of information on the most effective ways of relating to the reluctant. In this section, we offer six guidelines for reaching relationship-wary youth.[27] The subtitles suggest how youth might frame these ideas.

Connect in Times of Crisis: "Help Me, Don't Score Me"

Successful youth workers have long recognized that crisis can provide a turning point in strengthening relationships. In stressful situations, humans naturally reach out for support from trusted persons. At such times, the person is more vulnerable and receptive to attachment. Improperly handled, behavioral crises can increase conflict and alienation. But crisis events provide unique opportunities for teaching and relationship building. When the adult responds with sensitivity, bonds of trust strengthen. A high school teacher shared this example:

> Rob entered first period class ten minutes after the bell, and I asked for his late pass. He swore and stormed from the room.
>
> I stepped into the hall to confront his behavior but decided to connect by asking, "What's wrong, Rob?"
>
> "What's wrong!" he exclaimed. "I'm driving to school, and my car gets hit. After waiting for the police, I'm late. I get stopped in the hall by the principal. When I explain what happened, he

tells me to get to class. Now you send me out of class!" He whirled around starting toward the office.

"Where are you going?" I asked. "To get a pass!" he replied. "That's OK, Rob, enough has gone wrong for one day; you're welcome in class."

His hostility turned into a grateful apology, and we returned to class.[28]

Establish Rapid Trust: "You Seem Safe"

While building *relationships* can be a long and slow process, *connections* happen in the moment. Throughout human evolution, survival demanded the ability to make rapid gut-level decisions about whether a person is friend or foe.[29] Particularly in times of crisis, this brain system triggers social engagement or fight-or-flight reactions. Steve Van Bockern shares this experience:

> As I entered the office of a middle school, a teacher escorted an angry student to see the principal. *"All you ever do is lie, lie, lie—you know you knocked that book out of her hands on purpose!"* yelled the teacher. The student was trying to say it was an accident, but he was drowned out with more *"lies, lies, lies!"* The principal heard the heated exchange, directed the teacher to leave. She told the student to wait and went back into her office. I took the chair next to the sullen student and sat quietly for a moment before engaging the boy: *"We haven't met, but I just wanted you to know that you don't deserve to be talked to that way."* As we made eye contact, a tear rolled down his cheek.

The brain is designed to spot danger or safety using the *amygdala*, named for the Greek word for *almond*, which it resembles.[30] Located in each hemisphere of the emotional brain, the amygdala reads facial expression, tone of voice, and eye contact to make instant judgments of safety or threat. By monitoring our own emotional messages and those from the young person, we can help build trust.

Provide Fail-Safe Relationships: "Don't Give Up on Me"

Relational care is the foundation of success in any work with challenging youth.[31] This is not a touchy-feely truism but is based on decades of hard data from education, treatment, and positive youth development. Students who hate teachers and schools can only accept engagement from adults who can connect with them and kindle their innate desire for learning. Success in counseling and therapy is based less on technique than on the existence of a *helping alliance.*[32] Youth who become resilient and surmount unbelievable hardships are usually those who have bonded to positive adult models.

Long before science proved the power of relationships, pioneers in psychology and education discovered this through practical experience. In an 1829 book for teachers, Samuel R. Hall describes the unmatched power of connecting with students:

> If you succeed in gaining their love, your influence will be greater in some respects than that of parents themselves. It will be in your power to direct them into almost any path you choose . . . or, by your neglect they may become the reverse of everything that is lovely, amiable and generous.[33]

Increase Dosages of Nurturance: "I Need to Know You Care"

The person most in need of attachment is the one least likely to elicit support from others. Some even try to make themselves repugnant to fend off relationships. When encountering an "unlovable" person, one can visualize how the individual might have looked as a small child, thereby correcting a negative bias. Fritz Redl and David Wineman attacked the practice of withholding positive attention from children with bad behavior. Such youth desperately need love and affection whether they deserve it or not.[34] This is a central premise of what Louis Cozolino describes as *attachment-based teaching* since "supportive, encouraging, and caring relationships stimulate neural circuitry to learn."[35]

Some children may not be charismatic enough to naturally secure the nurturance they need from peers or adults. Children with less-engaging personalities don't find others lining up to build relationships with them. A child who is from a different economic or cultural background often feels ignored or rejected. Adults and young people need to take intentional action to reach out to troubled and traumatized individuals. As Bruce D. Perry and Maia Szalavitz note, "Relationships are the agents of change and the most powerful therapy is human love."[36]

Don't Crowd: "If You Get Too Close, I Will Back Away"

Children wary of adults are in an approach-avoidance conflict. They both crave and fear attachment. If adults crowd these youth, they will retreat. Building relationships with distrustful youth can be an endurance event. Trust develops in stages of casing, limit testing, and predictability.

- **Casing:** At the initial encounter, a youth experiences much uncertainty and has a need to check out the adult. The young person is diagnosing us by asking themselves: "Will this adult hurt me?" "Does this adult like me?" Children may suppress their normal behavioral responses during the casing stage, resulting in the *honeymoon* period. This initial period may be of short duration, but it gives the adult an opportunity to communicate acceptance and respect.

- **Limit testing:** After sufficiently scrutinizing the adult, the young person will need to test the waters. A child may be skeptical of the adult's friendly manner and reject bids for connection. Children may purposely misbehave or provoke the adult to see if this person is genuine or fake. A calm but firm approach is necessary to avoid either capitulating to the child or confirming that this is just another person not to be trusted.

- **Predictability:** The previous two stages provide a foundation for a more secure and stable relationship. This may or may not be an intimate connection, but both adult and child come to know what to expect from one another. Trust is a mutual process. The adult who conveys genuine like and trust for a youth will find those feelings reciprocated.

Trying to persuade a skeptical youth that "you can trust me" is likely to heighten distrust. It may be better to simply acknowledge, "I know you don't feel you can trust me yet, and that's all right." We trust when cumulative experiences prove that this adult is worth the risk. To trust is to become vulnerable, knowing one might be hurt or betrayed but feeling safe.

Model Respect to the Disrespectful: "Your Respect Builds Mine"

We respect others by treating them like we want to be treated—the essence of the Golden Rule. Being disrespected conveys the message that one is worthless. Disrespect triggers the emotion of shame, which easily converts into hatred. Persons who have experienced rejection and social exclusion are hyperalert to any communication that conveys disrespect. They read subtle cues to spot signs of dislike or rejection.

Many devalued groups are subjected to subtle *microinsults* as in acts of prejudice.[37] Insults have their sting by attacking another person's sense of self-worth. Clinician Kenneth V. Hardy describes the sense of devaluation resulting from racial trauma.[38] Profoundly devalued persons will do almost anything to gain respect. To some, death would be preferable to disrespect.

Some adults feel entitled to more respect than they demonstrate. They boss youth around, embarrass them in front of peers, and act in a condescending manner. Most disrespectful behavior is subtler, as when professionals patronize those they are pledged to serve. While adults may be unaware of their disrespect, young persons are not.

Schools *can* become sanctuaries of safety and Belonging. High school social science teacher John Odney had students grade their school using the Circle of Courage as a standard. Their diverse observations about Belonging were illuminating:

> Most of the faculty here really try to get to know you. It really makes me feel like I belong when a teacher calls me by my first name, even when I'm not in their class. . . .

> I was walking down the hall and I said hi to Mr. Nilson. He looked at me and said, "Oh, you're still here, you haven't dropped out yet."[39]

Every young person has a deep desire to belong. Children with the greatest unmet needs for relationships are often those most alienated from adults and peers. Schools and youth programs must make an intentional effort to nourish inviting relationships in a culture of Belonging.

CHAPTER 5

Brain-Friendly Learning: Strengthening Achievement

Children do not passively sit at desks waiting for information to be delivered and consumed. They are active explorers of their world.

—*Roberta M. Golinkoff and Kathy Hirsh-Pasek*[1]

Even within the first month of life, it is apparent that humans attempt to master their environments. Arms reach, fingers grasp, and eyes explore in search of meaning. Later, before stepping into a classroom, most children continue the innate search by learning the intricacies of language and playing challenging games. There is little sign of a limited attention span as they climb trees and play with friends.

Years pass, and skyscrapers, rockets, paintings, and cathedrals attest to the mind's continuing drive for creativity. But something happens to stifle the minds of many children who are eager to achieve—often in schools, which are supposed to kindle the spark for learning. Schooling can become noise that interrupts the natural flow of learning. A standardized curriculum fragments knowledge into subject areas, and assembly line education is the antithesis of how the brain learns. For centuries, reformers challenged hierarchical systems, as shown in this excerpt from the treatise *On the Education of Children* by Michel de Montaigne: "Tis the custom of schoolmasters to be eternally thundering in their pupils' ears as though they were pouring into a funnel, while the business of pupils is only to repeat what others have said before."[2]

The developing human brain is designed to mature slowly, downloading a culture over a period of two decades. Ironically, for thousands of years, Native peoples developed much more brain-friendly formats of learning. In a treatise on Indigenous education, Gregory Cajete describes this sophisticated pedagogical wisdom that emerged over millennia:[3]

- Experiential learning (learning by doing and seeing)
- Storytelling (learning by listening and imagining)
- Ritual and ceremony (learning through imitation)
- Dreaming (learning through unconscious imagery)
- Tutoring (learning through apprenticeship)
- Artistic reflection (learning through creative synthesis)

Such methods trump being tethered to textbooks and tests. Barbara Rogoff, Rebeca Mejía, and Maricela Correa-Chávez describe Western schooling as *assembly line instruction* while Indigenous societies employ *learning by observing and pitching in.*[4] Children learn through full participation in family and community endeavors.

We see the desire to master in all cultures from childhood onward. People explore, acquire language, construct things, and attempt to cope with their environments. The child who succeeds gains a strong feeling of pleasure, which fuels future motivation. Repeated failure has the opposite effect as the child learns to avoid challenging situations, curtailing the natural desire to achieve.[5]

The motivation to be competent permeates all physical, academic, and social realms. Students must balance the desire for mastery and the fear of failure. Some exert considerable effort, even on difficult tasks, to gain the pride of accomplishment. But for others, the fear of failure outweighs the motivation to achieve. We contend youth who have learned to expect failure escape further embarrassment and shame by working very hard at avoiding work. They challenge adults, endure punishment, and even drop out of school, having learned that failure is never as bitter if one does not try.

Although children need a preponderance of success, they also learn useful lessons from failure. Failure can provide *feedback* about what does not work and *motivation* for future success. "We have to think about failure as an opportunity rather than as a defeat."[6] We also need to teach children to fail courageously. In Samuel Beckett's words, "Try again, fail again, fail better."[7] The competent person will expect success but learn to surmount adversity. This is the core of resilience. Ernest Hemingway once wrote, "The world breaks everyone and afterwards many are strong at the broken places."[8]

Most traditional educational approaches emerged centuries before any scientific understanding of the human brain, but an explosion of neuroscience provides a blueprint for what we have called *deep-brain learning* that creates lasting change.[9] As Bruce D. Perry and Erin P. Hambrick note, "Without understanding the basic principles of how the brain develops and changes, we cannot expect to design and implement effective interventions."[10]

The Resilient Brain

One of the most exciting findings in brain science is the concept of *neuroplasticity*—*neuro* refers to brain cells, and *plastic* means malleable. *Neuroplasticity* is the ability of the brain to change itself in the face of new problems and opportunities.[11] Neuroplasticity can be for better or for worse—experience designs brain pathways for resilience as well as for reactive coping strategies.[12] The brain also designs new circuits to compensate for damage.[13]

Adolescence is a remarkable period of neuroplasticity as brains are much more reactive to external forces. There is nothing deficient about teen brains. Nature did not design the young for independent decision making. Throughout history, children and adolescents grew to maturity in the presence of elders and more responsible peers. Only in the modern era do youth spend their formative years socialized by peers in the absence of consistent adult influences, including both teachers and parents.[14]

The modern juvenile court formed in the United States in 1899 with the recognition that adolescent problems do not predict a lifetime of problem behavior. But over the 20th century, courts became more punitive, and large numbers of youth were incarcerated with some sentenced to life without parole.[15] In the 21st century, subsequent Supreme Court decisions, based on evidence that adolescent brain development differs from adults, are beginning to curtail these practices.[16] Research shows that teen brains are less capable of self-regulation, have less capacity for mature judgment, are less able to foresee long-term consequences of behavior, and are vulnerable to negative influences and peer approval.[17] Although the quest for excitement is natural among teens, an experiential and adventurous education can help them channel this excitement into productive activities.[18]

Genes Are Not Destiny

The nature versus nurture debate is over—it's both. The science of *epigenetics* shows how nurture changes genes. *Epi* is Greek for *on top of*, and epigenetics shows how environment shapes *genes*.[19] DNA does not determine our destiny.

Our entire set of forty-six chromosomes with twenty thousand genes is packed in the nucleus of virtually all our trillions of bodily cells. Yet, genes make up less than 5 percent of human chromosomes, with even experts often referring to the rest as *junk DNA*. The stunning discovery: so-called junk DNA contains a treasure trove of hidden switches that shape life destiny.[20]

Beginning in the fetal stage, signals from the environment can turn genes on or off. A massive study called ENCODE has mapped four million *gene switches* that enable the body and brain to adapt to our unique environments.[21] Gene expression can change through love or abuse, serenity or stress, positive thoughts or pessimistic fears, and healthy or unhealthy diets.[22]

Our *epigenome* has evolved to meet challenges humans have repeatedly encountered over history. For example, humans have had periodic famine throughout history, so there are epigenetic switches in pregnant women to alter metabolism so a newborn will need less food. This was one outcome of forced starvation in the Dutch Hunger Winter during World War II.[23]

Complicating normal development is global industry, which has produced over 83,000 chemicals not natural in human history.[24] In some cases, exposure can create wildly unpredictable effects on health and growth. This chemical roulette is related to aggressiveness, learning problems, and more. A growing concern is that many so-called side effects of psychiatric medications may be adverse epigenetic wild cards.[25]

What's most important for our purposes is the role epigenetics plays in building resilient brains. The Allen Institute of Brain Science finds that 84 percent of all human genes impact the growth and development of the brain.[26] Healthy experiences build resilience. Manageable levels of stress can have a steeling effect, preparing us to cope with future difficulties.[27] But, overwhelming traumatic events signal genes to set our stress systems on high alert. Thus, physical and sexual abuse, cold parenting, and chaos in the home can produce epigenetic disruption in both brain and body.[28] An example is the study of lifelong effects of adverse childhood experiences, which are traumatic events such as abuse or neglect, that show causative connections with physical and mental health problems throughout a person's life.[29]

Canadian researcher Michael J. Meaney of McGill University finds that nurturing caregiving creates resilient, emotionally stable off-spring. In contrast, his research finds that maternal neglect alters the expression of genes necessary to calm stress—producing hypervigilant, anxious offspring.[30]

It doesn't stop there. Trauma earlier generations experienced can influence the structure of our genes, making them more likely to switch on negative responses to stress and trauma. Epigenetic changes abound during the fetal stage, when an average of 250,000 new neurons are created each minute throughout pregnancy.[31] For tens of thousands of years, Indigenous peoples already believed that experiences of the pregnant mother affect characteristics of her offspring. The intergenerational effects of trauma were widely known in Indigenous cultures, which used elaborate means to protect pregnant women from stressful experiences.[32]

Although environment can trigger negative epigenetic changes, new experiences can reverse them. However, some effects persist for up to three or four generations. This explains the cross-generational effects of cultural trauma.[33] Entire social systems can be disrupted through epigenetics.[34]

Some children are genetically more vulnerable to epigenetic influences. Those with *timid temperaments* are highly reactive to maltreatment, while those with *bold temperaments* are less reactive.[35] Yet high reactivity is not a flaw, since life experiences more strongly influence reactive children, for better or worse. Thus, they respond more negatively to rejection and maltreatment but also more positively to warmth and acceptance. They thrive with supportive relationships.

In contrast, less reactive youth are more insulated from environmental influences.[36]

Although harmful experiences trigger epigenetic changes, subsequent positive experiences can also alleviate these. This is not a cure-all, as research on Romanian orphans shows that some epigenetic effects of extreme deprivation are not readily reversible.[37] Still, neuroplasticity gives the capacity to build new brain circuits to work around the traces of trauma. This new science demonstrates the profound benefits healthy environments have on learning, behavior, and growth.

Safety and Learning

Humans are strongly motivated to stay safe—but taking risks is essential for healthy growth and development. In order to thrive, children must balance safety with *adventure*—which is defined as *taking risks*.[38] As John Shedd says, "A ship in harbor is safe, but that is not what ships are built for."[39]

Safety is in the eye of the beholder as only individuals can determine *felt safety*. This includes physical, emotional, relational, and cultural safety.[40] The opposite of safety is feeling threatened or frightened. In the face of threat, calm adults help children restore a sense of safety. But if distress is overwhelming—or if caregivers themselves are the source of danger—children have no way to calm their fear.[41]

In any given moment, we have two options: to step forward into growth, or to step back into safety.

—*Abraham H. Maslow*[42]

The need for safety motivates much of human behavior. This is not just protection from extreme harm, but also from subtle threats to one's sense of self-worth. The lack of safety drives emotions of anxiety, fear, loss, and shame. Whether child or adult, all need to feel safe from hurt or humiliation.

In the presence of threat, primitive survival reactions highjack higher rational brain circuits.[43] The potential for threat permeates the school experience. It emanates from teachers, other students, testing, curriculum, and the climate of the school itself.

Many safe-school practices, such as zero tolerance and heavy police presence, do nothing to foster feelings of safety. As Linda Lantieri observes, "An ounce of prevention is worth a pound of metal detectors."[44] Likewise, schools often rationalize seclusion and restraint as safety procedures with troubled children but only create more risk.

Another threat comes from imposing irrelevant and uninteresting curriculum and textbooks. The brain tunes out information it considers pointless. The proliferation of children labeled with *attention deficit disorders* might better be conceptualized as *interest deficit disorders* in the curriculum. Many of these children with so-called attention deficits are very actively attending, but to something the brain finds more novel and adventuresome than textbook trivia.

Stressed adults are not equipped to create calm and safe environments for children.[45] Nearly half of U.S. teachers report encountering a large amount of daily stress—tied with nurses as the most stressful professions.[46] Our stressful existence has fueled a proliferation of publications on meditation and mindfulness activities, both for adults and young people.[47] There are a variety of mindful instructional practices to help engage students in their own learning.[48]

A survey of preadolescents shows that two of the top three sources of stress are school related, including grades and homework, family stress, and peer relationships. Students report they manage stress with recreation, music, television or video games, and conversations with friends. None of the top ten coping strategies in the survey involve being contemplative.[49]

Although formal mindfulness training may reduce stress, the most direct means of prevention is a safe living and learning environment. As psychologist and trauma expert Louis Cozolino notes, for most of the last one hundred thousand years, humans lived in small bands of mutual support. Family members and tribal elders carried the responsibility of teaching, and children learned in environments of safety and secure attachment. He calls for creating a *tribal classroom* organized around how our brains evolve to learn: "Children learn best when they feel connected, appreciated, and safe. The goal of attachment-based teaching is for each child to move from feeling vulnerable, frightened, and unimportant to feeling protected, cared for, and valued."[50]

For youth who have experienced mistreatment by adults or peers, a secure family and school environment is the first step to healing. Child trauma expert Bruce Perry suggests specific *safety strategies* for parents and educators.[51]

- **Physically nurture young children:** Although touch is a mainstay of parenting, this issue may be unsettling to some professionals. Still, small children may need safe touch to feel secure. With those who have a history of physical or sexual abuse, one must be attuned and carefully monitor how they respond. The online journal *Thriving* provides a review of research and practice issues concerning touch.[52]

- **Treat children based on emotional age:** When fearful or frustrated, a ten-year-old may regress and become like a toddler. This calls for using soothing nonverbal interactions as one would use with a small child. Children in distress are not equipped to begin logical problem-solving communication. Instead, the adult must communicate an aura of calmness which sets the stage for later opportunities to discuss problem events.

- **Be consistent and predictable:** Abrupt changes in schedules, transitions, and sometimes even surprises and celebrations can trigger feelings of unsafety. When anxious and insecure, children cannot self-regulate and need help calming the fight-or-flight survival brain. Chaos is unsettling, and children need the security of an environment where the adult is in authoritative control.

In their book, *The Three Pillars of Care*, Howard Bath and John R. Seita describe strategies for fostering *safety*, *connections*, and *coping* to build resilience with children of trauma.[53] Seita, himself a former youth at risk, is a professor at Michigan State University. He recalls this personal experience as an angry thirteen-year-old encountering his teacher:

> I remember struggling with composing a sentence in English class. Boiling with frustration and close to rage, I crumpled up a page and flung it towards the teacher, Mr. U. who deftly caught it. He walked toward me smiling. "Nice throw, what's up?" he asked. "I can't do this crap, it's stupid," I replied. "Maybe it seems that way" said Mr. U., "but you can do it, and we'll do it together, OK?"
>
> Mr. U. sat down next to me, gently and calmly helping me compose the sentence. In the scheme of my early life, this was a relatively minor event; but decades later, I still recall this episode where the teacher chose to co-regulate with me rather than punish me for my provocative behavior.[54]

Experiential Learning

John Dewey's epic *Democracy and Education* proposes a blueprint for schools that is still applicable in modern-day classrooms.[55] His premise is that the most powerful learning is experiential. These are principles that modern neuroscience and research on learning and development fully validate. However, many presume that hands-on activities and practical courses are less important than a traditional *rigorous* academic curriculum—but the brain demands *relevance*.[56] Experiential activities are essential to engage disinterested students and provide learning that transfers to real-life settings.[57]

We only think when we have a problem.

—*John Dewey*[58]

Dewey saw schools as microcosms of democracy. These embryonic communities would reflect the best ideals of the larger society, developing practical skills as well as academic learning, and enlivened by the arts:

> When the school introduces and trains each child of society into membership in such a little community, saturating him with the spirit of service, and providing him with the instruments of effective self-direction, we shall have the deepest and best guaranty of a larger society which is worthy, lovely, and harmonious.[59]

Schools in a democracy should teach children how to think, not what to think, says Dewey. This requires a rediscovery of the power of *learning by doing*. The 3rd century BC Confucian philosopher Xunzi captured this truism:

> I hear and I forget.
> I see and I remember.
> I do and I understand.[60]

Dewey saw solving problems as more important than storing knowledge. Think of how we keep wrestling with unresolved situations even during sleep and dreams (the Zeigarnik effect).[61] When not facing problems, we invent them, working on puzzles, hobbies, and challenging activities. But traditional education often keeps students in a passive role, being fed a canned curriculum.

Perhaps the best examples of brain-friendly learning emanate from experience-based philosophies. Though called by many names—experiential education, adventure education, and project-based learning—all strive to make learning active, interesting, relevant, and challenging.

This is particularly noteworthy given modern emphasis on *high-stakes testing*, which corrupts education by stifling intrinsic learning.[62] As instruction tunnels in on tested topics, curriculum stagnates and students at risk disengage from learning.[63] In contrast, self-testing is a powerful learning tool. For example, cramming to review is less effective than taking a practice test; the latter builds brain pathways for retrieving memories.[64] Thus, testing that provides feedback (not just grading performance) is a powerful memory builder.[65]

While learning by doing is not common in many conventional schools, it has a rich tradition in alternative education and youth development. Young brains are primed to seek stimulation, and intense, novel experiences spike brain-cell growth.[66] Placing youth in challenging new settings can disrupt old patterns and motivate their learning.

Schools concerned with mastery provide alternative strategies for students who are not experiencing success. "When children fail in ways that discourage and remove the learning spark, it gives reason for staff to ask why and then adapt and try something different."[67]

How do we rekindle the spark of learning? John G. Nicholls describes two contrasting motives for achievement, egoistic and task motivation:[68]

> *Egoistic motivation: I want to be better than others.* Although competition may be a motivator, it can also undermine creativity and problem-solving ability. Youth who fear failure may avoid difficult challenges and show helplessness or problem behavior.
>
> *Task motivation: I want to do my best.* The focus is on learning rather than being preoccupied with the need to impress others.

> Being engaged in a challenging task is called *flow* as the brain
> is on a roll searching for solutions.[69]

In her book *Grit*, Angela Duckworth provides evidence that IQ and natural talent do not drive success.[70] She describes how her father, a scientist, belittled his daughter's lack of genius. He was furious when she chose to work with children rather than pursue medical school. But inspired in college by work with disadvantaged students, she found a purpose for her life career. Ironically, this girl who supposedly lacked genius would receive a MacArthur Fellowship genius grant. It is worth noting that, when she finished writing *Grit*, she went to visit her father who was then disabled by Parkinson's disease. She read the entire book to him line by line; when she finished, he nodded and smiled.

The brain becomes intelligent by mastering difficulty. Persons who gain high levels of expertise in any area have developed brain circuits that are hundreds of times more efficient than those of a novice. Carol S. Dweck shows that achievement is strongly related to one's personal belief about the following two mindsets.[71]

1. **Fixed mindset:** This mindset considers intelligence an inherited trait that a person either has or doesn't have. People with fixed mindsets often avoid risking failure and give up in the face of difficulty.
2. **Growth mindset:** With this mindset, an individual believes intelligence derives from hard work. It encourages mistakes as a vehicle for learning and provides the confidence necessary to take on difficult tasks.

Dweck developed a *Brainology* workshop to teach children how to build their intelligence:

> The more that you challenge your mind to learn, the more
> your brain cells grow. Then, things that you once found very

hard or even impossible—like speaking a foreign language or
doing algebra—seem to become easy. The result is a stronger,
smarter brain.[72]

After a Brainology workshop, Jimmy, a struggling student came
to her with tears in his eyes: "You mean I don't have to be dumb?"[73]
One can build a growth mindset by teaching students that talent is
developed, not controlled by genes. Conversely, when an adult does
not believe in the potential of young people, it becomes hard for
them to rise above those low expectations.

The neuroscience revolution has unleashed a flood of questionable
promotions for online programs to rewire your brain and raise intelligence. While practice improves performance, "there is very little
evidence that brain training products lead to what psychologists call
transfer effects."[74] It is not gadgets and games that rewire the brain
for learning but life experiences. Sustained tasks like learning a language, music, and motor skills strengthen brain pathways making
the activity automated and effortless. We rewire our brains with rich
social interaction, not contrived curricula.

Learning Is Social

From the beginning of human community, the brain has made
use of conversation and oral stories as primary formats for learning.
Since life itself takes the shape of a narrative, it makes sense that the
brain would specialize in that form. Around a campfire or a kitchen
table, stories are etched in the brain. In contrast to conversation and
dialogue, lecture and recitation are the primary currency of exchange
in Western schools.

*A good way to keep your brain "oiled" is simply to spend time
talking with people.*

—Andy Zynga[75]

Perhaps the most underused potential of the brain is to tap the power of groups in conversation. Typical classroom discussions are a series of two-person interactions with the instructor weighing in after each contribution from a student. Real dialogue allows all who want to join the conversation to contribute; students respond to one another, not just to the teacher in control. This genuine discourse requires that students learn to listen to one another and share competing or complementary ideas in a climate of respect.[76] Such is how the brain evolved over thousands of years in egalitarian cultures.

Adult-Child Relationships

A central theme in research is the importance of adult-child relationships to growth and development. Science is validating what youth-work pioneers have long known. Yet, as Mark Smith of the University of Edinburgh notes, youth workers have been trained to keep a professional distance. He cites pioneering educator Pestalozzi who saw love as essential to teaching if the physical and intellectual powers of the child are to develop: "Yet in the current climate love is a word that can ring alarm bells when applied to the care of other people's children."[77]

Throughout human history, the most important learning has taken place in social settings. The human brain is designed to function better in social interaction than in isolation. Highly competitive schools become an individualistic *I win, you lose* game. By nurturing social, emotional, and academic competence, all students can rise together.

Social-emotional learning is not an optional add-on to the curriculum, but the foundation for successful learning and positive life outcomes.[78] The most powerful impact comes not from some formal evidence-based curriculum but by creating a climate of belonging and respect. Research on resilience shows that when children are lacking stable and supportive relationships at home, the school can nurture these unmet needs. Figure 5.1 (page 80) illustrates how a

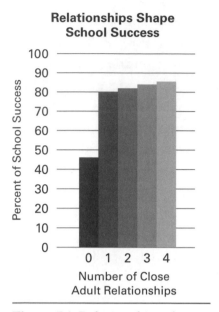

Relationships Shape School Success

Number of Close Adult Relationships

Figure 5.1: Relationships shape school success.

close supportive bond with an adult is a potent predictor of school success.[79] With no close adult relationship, less than half of students succeed in school, but just one close bond raises the success rate to 80 percent.

Cooperative Learning

Cooperative learning between peers produces a powerful synergy because it addresses each of the Circle of Courage needs. Students work in small social groups fostering Belonging. Learning together enhances Mastery. Students are not passive recipients of information but develop Independence by taking responsibility for their learning. Finally, helping others strengthens Generosity.

Cooperative learning enhances these aspects of motivation and group cohesion.[80] In a variation called *Teams, Games, and Tournaments*, students play academic games instead of taking quizzes.[81] This and other research indicate that such forms of cooperative learning can increase academic performance with students at risk.[82] Both group performance and individual achievement are assessable.

The benefits of cooperative learning, in contrast to competition or individual learning, are well-documented. Students' attitudes toward teachers and peers become more positive, and students develop increased prosocial abilities (such as empathy and altruism) and social skills (such as communication and conflict management). Even if computers are used in learning, cooperative instruction enhances motivation and achievement.[83]

Given the evidence of its effectiveness, several factors have limited the adoption of cooperative learning. Many educators teach the way they were taught, which did not include students learning from students. Others shy away from cooperative learning because they have seen it improperly used in chaotic classrooms. Some are not aware that learning itself is an inherently social activity. Cooperative learning challenges ingrained myths of individualism or competition— believing strong individuals succeed without the help of others.

We believe all youth have within them an internal desire to achieve, but when the Circle of Courage is broken, Mastery can feel unattainable, particularly so for youth at risk. This often leads to fear of failure and rejection of learning. Traditional learning practices exacerbate this to the detriment of all students, but particularly those at greatest risk.

To counteract these effects and tap the resiliency inherent in all children, educators and youth-work practitioners can provide an environment of physical and emotional safety where youth can learn from failure and work with trusted adults and peers toward success. We close this chapter with an inspiring account of cooperative learning from social psychologist Elliot Aronson.

Brain-Friendly Learning in Action

Aronson developed a creative system for cooperative learning called the *jigsaw classroom* (https://jigsaw.org). Students work in small groups where each participant contributes one piece of the task and teaches it to peers. Jigsaw has a four-decade record of positive educational outcomes including improved test performance, reduced absenteeism, greater liking for school, and reduced racial conflict.[84] Aronson provides the following description, condensed from the website:

> The jigsaw classroom was first used in Austin, Texas when
> White, African-American, and Hispanic youngsters were placed

in integrated classrooms. Long-standing fear and distrust produced an atmosphere of turmoil and hostility. After observing what was going on in classrooms for a few days, my students and I concluded that inter-group hostility was being fueled by the climate of the classroom.

We realized that we needed to shift the emphasis from a relentlessly competitive atmosphere to a more cooperative one. Our first intervention was with fifth graders. We helped several teachers devise a cooperative jigsaw structure for the students to learn about the life of Eleanor Roosevelt. We divided the students into small groups, diversified in terms of race, ethnicity and gender, making each student responsible for a specific part of Roosevelt's biography. At least one or two of the students in each group were already viewed as "losers" by their classmates.

Carlos was one such student, very shy and insecure in his new surroundings. English was his second language. After attending an inadequately funded, substandard neighborhood school consisting entirely of Hispanic students like himself, he was suddenly catapulted into a class with Anglo students who spoke English fluently, seemed to know much more than he did, and who were not reluctant to let him know it.

When we restructured the classroom so that students were now working together in small groups, this was initially terrifying to Carlos. He was still reluctant to speak when it was his turn to teach the students in his jigsaw group. He blushed, stammered, and had difficulty covering the material he had learned. Skilled in the ways of the competitive classroom, the other students were quick to ridicule him with comments such as, "You're stupid. You don't know what you're doing. You can't even speak English."

Within a few days of working with jigsaw, Carlos's group-mates gradually realized that they needed to change their tactics. It was no longer in their own best interest to rattle Carlos; they needed him to perform well in order to do well themselves. After a week or two, most of Carlos's group-mates developed into skillful interviewers, asking him relevant questions and helping him articulate clear answers. And as Carlos succeeded, his group-mates began to see him in a more positive light. Carlos saw himself as a competent member of the class and his group-mates as friendly and supportive. School became a more humane, exciting place.[85]

The effects of cooperative learning were shown a decade after this experience when Aronson received this letter from Carlos:

Dear Professor Aronson:

I am a senior at University of Texas. Today I got a letter admitting me to the Harvard Law School. You are probably wondering why this stranger is writing to you and bragging about his achievements. You see, last year I was taking a course in social psychology and we were using a book you wrote, *The Social Animal*, and when I read about prejudice and jigsaw it all sounded very familiar—and then, I realized that I was in that very first class you ever did jigsaw in—when I was in the 5th grade. And as I read on, it dawned on me that I was the boy that you called Carlos.

I remembered when you first came to our classroom how I was scared and hated school and how I was so stupid and didn't know anything. When we started to do work in jigsaw groups, I began to realize that I wasn't really that stupid. And the kids I thought were cruel and hostile became my friends and the teacher acted friendly and nice to me. I actually began to love school and learn and now I'm about to go to Harvard Law School.

My mother tells me that when I was born, I almost died. I was born at home and the cord was wrapped around my neck and the midwife gave me mouth to mouth and saved my life. If she was still alive, I would write to her too, to tell her that I grew up smart and good and I'm going to law school. But she died a few years ago. I'm writing to you because, no less than her, you saved my life too.

Sincerely,
Carlos[86]

CHAPTER 6

Pathways to Responsibility: Strengthening Autonomy

We must aim at cultivating the will, not breaking it.
—Maria Montessori[1]

Anthropologist Ruth Benedict describes how traditional Native American cultures give young children real opportunities for responsibility that foster Independence and treat them as social equals.[2] In contrast, contemporary societies often exclude youth from responsible participation and then decry their lack of responsibility.

Polish educational pioneer Janusz Korczak founded a school for street children on the principle of *pedocracy*, where students are empowered through a system of self-governance. He saw children not as future citizens but citizens in embryo. Korczak penned a children's book, *King Matt the First*, describing a twelve-year-old boy who becomes monarch. The boy king leads children who march forth under a green flag to reform a world corrupted by adults.[3]

Research on resilience indicates that responsibility requires using one's power to meet the needs of both self and others.[4] Young people who don't feel in charge of their destiny are tossed like a rudderless boat on a stormy sea, buffeted by life's difficulties. They act in ways that harm themselves or turn their pain outward and hurt others. But as they take responsibility for their behavior, they can begin to change the direction of their lives.

Understanding Autonomy

The human brain is designed for *autonomy*, the need to assert personal power and resist coercion. Daniel H. Pink observes that autonomy is not independence in the sense of "I'll go it alone" individualism. *Genuine autonomy* means acting with self-control while still being interdependent with others. As they mature, children show an increasing need to be independent and free.[5]

If what we are doing for children is so good for them, why do they fight us so much?

—Roderick Durkin[6]

Children respond in different ways when their autonomy is blocked. Although some are compliant, others feel unfairly treated and strongly resist control. Children are less likely to internalize values that are externally imposed. By providing opportunities to exercise influence over their own lives, adults encourage the development of self-discipline.

The quest for autonomy is present even in toddlers and increases with maturity. Infants are totally dependent. They must learn to cope by increasingly managing *internal* emotions and impulses as well as *external* challenges and threats.[7] They also must use their power responsibly, respecting the rights of others. This involves *self-control*, *self-confidence*, and *shared responsibility*.

Self-Control

Self-control is the first step on the pathway to responsibility. In the words of Holocaust survivor Elie Wiesel, "Ultimately, the only power to which man should aspire is that which he exercises over himself."[8] Self-control is learned as a caregiver meets an infant's needs and calms distress. In effect, children borrow the emotionally stable adult brain. Mirror neurons enable the child to match the adult's more serene state and shut down stress reactions. After thousands of such interactions, the child develops the capacity to self-calm.

Mature self-regulation requires building circuits in the higher executive brain, which is a two-decade process. When a child has experienced relational trauma or has a reactive temperament, self-regulation is the first casualty.[9]

While it seems natural to calm a distressed child, one can easily be drawn into conflict with an agitated youth who supposedly should know better or seems to be purposely misbehaving. Still, like the small child, older youth also learn self-regulation by interacting with the calm brain of a caring person. A sure way to make problems worse is to scream in the face of an upset child, "Calm down!" Children or teens who are still struggling to develop self-control need persons who help them calm, a process called *coregulation*.[10] Table 6.1 shows this.

Table 6.1: Coercive Control Versus Coregulation

Coercion	Coregulation
Controlling the person	Calming the person
Using a harsh aggressive tone	Using a soothing confident tone
Venting one's own feelings	Managing one's own feelings
Reacting to problems	Responding to needs

Self-Confidence

Self-confidence is essential in developing mature responsibility. Children develop a sense of personal power as they discover they can control their world to meet their needs. Albert Bandura coined the term *self-efficacy* as the power within, the sense of being in charge of one's destiny.[11] He notes that persons who have the same set of skills may have dramatically different performance because of beliefs about their personal power. As children mature, they normally gain an increased sense of power as they influence their world to meet their needs.

The opposite of self-efficacy is learned helplessness, which leads to feelings of defeat and depression.[12] Powerlessness also profoundly affects levels of stress chemicals in the brain and body.[13] Sometimes, instead of retreating in impotence, youth stripped of power react with opposition (helplessness) or rebellion.

- *Helplessness* is seen in the mindset, "Nothing I do will make a difference." These youth desire control but believe it is futile to try to assert power. They feel like pawns dominated by others and lack the courage to master challenges. Helplessness puts youth at risk for a host of emotional and behavioral difficulties.

- *Rebellion* is expressed in the mindset, "Nobody is going to tell me what to do." Youth exert power through purposely oppositional behavior, rule breaking, and joining an antisocial group. British psychologist Denis Stott describes how some flaunt their badness by "going to the devil" to assert their power.[14] They derive a false sense of pride by defying others.

How do we counter the sense of impotence or defiance that characterizes powerless youth? Despite decades of programs purporting to build self-esteem in youth, most programs ignore the fact that self-worth is a result of meeting developmental needs, not a goal in itself. Stanley Coopersmith recognizes this in his classic study, *The Antecedents of Self-Esteem*.[15] With concepts that parallel the Circle of Courage, young people develop self-worth as they experience significance (being important to someone), competence (being skilled at something), power (controlling one's destiny), and virtue (contributing to others). Unless these needs are all in balance, life itself is not in balance.

Shared Responsibility

Shared responsibility is the only way all members of a community can meet their needs for autonomy. David D. Wills, who pioneered schools for *wayward adolescents* in Great Britain, saw *shared responsibility* as an inalienable right of youth in a democracy.[16] Alfred Adler describes *equality* as an ironclad law governing social interactions—just as gravity governs physical bodies. Without social equality, there can be no harmony.[17] This does not mean equal ability but equal rights and needs. Despite individual differences, all are entitled to dignity and respect.[18]

Although some are better able to influence others, everyone has an inborn need to exercise power. Ukrainian youth-work pioneer Anton S. Makarenko made sure that all students had opportunities to lead as well as to follow—both essential skills for living in a social community.[19] Since different tasks call for different abilities, all youth will eventually face the responsibility of leadership. Thus, the most valuable leaders are those committed to the well-being of others, which is the principle of servant leadership.[20]

Kurt Lewin was the founder of modern social psychology. He studied three styles of leadership adults often exercise when working with children's groups: authoritarian, permissive, and democratic.[21] He finds the following.

- Groups with autocratic leaders were productive only when an adult supervised them; peer dynamics were riddled with bullying.

- Permissive leaders were disengaged from children, which eroded adult influence and produced chaotic groups.

- Democratic leaders formed groups where peers supported one another and kept on task even in the absence of the leader.

Aligning with these styles, moral development researcher Martin L. Hoffman describes three patterns of discipline adults often use: (1) *power assertion*, (2) *love withdrawal*, and (3) *problem solving*.[22] Although power assertion may sometimes be necessary, youth fail to develop moral values. Love withdrawal is emotional neglect, as it jeopardizes the most basic need of children for belonging. Problem solving engages youth in evaluating their behavior. Discipline problems become opportunities for growth. Daily life experiences are teachable moments to develop responsibility and self-discipline.[23]

Rethinking Discipline

The history of discipline in Western civilization is a litany of futile attempts to compel obedience. In 1877, Italian youth-work pioneer John Bosco described the perpetual conflict between forces of kindness (preventative) and punishment (repressive).[24] The progressive 19th century moral treatment movement in psychiatry gave way to physical and chemical restraint. No-tolerance schools replaced progressive education. The juvenile courts created to rehabilitate the youth would regress into retribution. There are always advocates for these polarized views, which are shaped by cultural experience and the human brain.

The rise of Hitler gave rise to research on the authoritarian personality relative to democratic leadership.[25] Since the terms *authoritarian* and *nonauthoritarian* embody strong biases, we will replace these with more positive labels. Authoritarian values emphasize *responsibility*; nonauthoritarian values place high priority on *freedom*. When times are good, humans live in harmony embracing both responsibility and freedom. In threatening times, many give up freedom in search for a strong leader.[26]

There are two systems which have been in use through all ages in educating youth: the preventive and repressive.

—*John Bosco*[27]

There are natural brain-based differences in tendencies toward freedom or responsibility. These personality patterns are tied to reactivity of the amygdala, as well as levels of oxytocin, the trust and bonding chemical.[28] Responsibility types are conscientious about rules and stability while those disposed toward freedom embrace flexibility and change. Humans survived for millennia by maintaining a balance between these differences.

Personality differences shape philosophies of discipline. Stanley Feldman and Karen Stenner formulated four neutral questions about child-rearing values which reliably measure whether persons are more inclined to freedom or responsibility.[29] As the following list demonstrates, there is no right or wrong answer, as all options have positive qualities. *Which is more important?*

1. Independence or respect for elders
2. Obedience or self-reliance
3. To be considerate or well-behaved
4. Curiosity or good manners

Responsibility mindsets endorse respect for elders, obedience, being well-behaved, and having good manners. In contrast, freedom mindsets elevate independence, self-reliance, being considerate, and curiosity. But effective education and youth work requires a balance of freedom *and* responsibility.[30]

Parenting Styles

Developmental psychologist Diana Baumrind conducted key studies on parenting.[31] Her findings apply to all who are involved in socialization of children. Researchers carefully observed family interactions in the home and laboratory from the time children entered preschool through high school. Another study examined peer relations and school performance as children grew to maturity. Parents showed notably different approaches in warmth and control.[32] Baumrind identifies three main parenting styles.

1. **Permissive:** While permissive adults may want to respond to the needs of the young person, they fail to set expectations such as following rules or respecting others. When children test limits, permissive adults avoid confrontation, perhaps wanting to be friends rather than authority figures. Their children show less self-regulation and responsibility and greater risk for drug use. Another variation occurs with neglectful adults who are low in both warmth and control.

2. **Authoritarian:** In contrast to permissive figures, these adults are demanding but unresponsive. They lack warmth or tenderness and show little respect for the young person's views. To instill obedience, they use threats, punishments, or bribes rather than communication. Children reared in this manner display fewer academic skills, give in to peer pressure, and have more adjustment problems such as anxiety, depression, or defiance.

3. **Authoritative:** These adults balance freedom and control. They set demands and meet needs. They monitor the youth's activities but are warm and understanding.

Discipline may at times be confrontive but not coercive. When they must assert power, they use communication to help youth see how their behavior affects others. Children live in harmony with adults, do well in school, and seek prosocial peers.

These are only prototypes of parenting, since the real world is more complex. Even in the same family, children with different temperaments may need more controlling or nurturing styles. Cultural differences also shape parenting, and educators must be aware of these differences when working with students. Chinese parents tend to be more strict than North American parents, and their authoritative parenting produces better social and school performance in their children.[33] African American parents in high-crime communities may be more authoritarian, but this may be to protect their children rather than wield control.

The desire for greater autonomy is a core characteristic of child and adolescent development. Yet, while the quest for autonomy increases dramatically, opportunities for decision making and self-determination do not.[34] This imbalance can fuel cross-generation conflict—adults struggle for control, while youth strive to run their own lives. Student engagement is a key to school success, yet students routinely describe themselves as disengaged. Research shows that students who perceive their classrooms as encouraging autonomy become more engaged in learning.[35]

University of Michigan researchers studied the impact of autonomy on the effectiveness of group treatment programs for teens. They measured autonomy with questions that gauged whether "staff give students responsibility" or "staff order the students around." Young people who saw themselves as autonomous were more supportive of program goals. The group climate was more safe, orderly, and humane.[36] The concept of empowering youth is widely touted but underutilized. We empower children when we guide them toward better decision making and more constructive behavior.[37]

Youth deprived of autonomy often form negative countercultures. "Building walls makes wall-climbing a sport," said German youth-work pioneer Otto Zirker.[38] Authoritarian control becomes self-perpetuating: the more one controls, the more one needs to control. Autocratic adults believe they are creating an organized environment; the actual result is an underground youth culture of conflict and chaos. In contrast, democratic group climates develop autonomy by engaging youth in responsible roles and building a sense of shared community.[39]

A common misunderstanding in discussions about autonomy is the notion one is advocating complete freedom. Adults who grant freedom without guidance are sending youth on a journey without a map. Young people need clear and consistent expectations in order to successfully navigate life's challenges. Instead of being preoccupied with control, adults map out the structure and values. Youth in this environment develop responsible independence, while adults still exert major influence.

Discipline Versus Punishment

All child-rearing involves some assertion of the power of adults over their young. In the purest form of discipline, an adult provides a positive model and values to guide a young disciple. But this concept has mutated so that dictionaries also define *discipline* as a synonym of *punishment*. Table 6.2 contrasts these concepts. Discipline is a process of teaching, not of coercion. It seeks to develop social responsibility and self-control. The exercise of adult coercion and control impedes discipline.[40]

The word *discipline* has roots in the Latin word *disciplina*, meaning education to produce self-control. Jean-Jacques Rousseau proposes that "punishment must never be inflicted on children, but it should

Table 6.2: Redefining Discipline

Discipline	Punishment
1. Teach to prevent future problems.	1. Use pain to penalize past behavior.
2. Develop respect and social responsibility.	2. Develop obedience to authority.
3. Discuss natural consequences.	3. Administer arbitrary consequences.
4. Strengthen internal prosocial values.	4. Impose external rule enforcement.
5. Strengthen empathy circuits in the brain.	5. Condition pain circuits in the brain.

always happen to them as a natural consequence of their bad action."[41] Instead of punishing for lying, he proposes a youth must learn of the bad effects of lying such as not being trusted or believed when one tells the truth. Such interactions turn problems into learning opportunities and foster moral development.[42]

Natural consequences are powerful when available. But if not, then as Rudolf Dreikurs, Bernice Bronia Grunwald, and Floyd C. Pepper suggest, consequences should at least be logical.[43] This could also be seen as an example of what is now known as *restorative justice—* repairing harm instead of administering punishment.[44]

Children can never be effectively socialized if the balance of interventions are more punitive than positive. Punishment should come from caring adults who use it occasionally and judiciously. Punishment has a destructive effect if a child perceives it as rejection from adults who should provide love and security. We suggest the following guidelines for genuine discipline, which shifts the focus from administering consequences to instilling responsibility.

- **Going from rules to values:** It is a truism that children have to learn to live by the rules, but preoccupation with rules should not obscure values. Rule books may make those in power feel secure, but if frontline staff and youth do not own those rules, they are likely to ignore them. Effective schools for youth at risk adapt flexibly to the needs of students rather than make every decision by the book. Rigid procedures turn professionals into clerks and technocrats. Programs that shift from pursuing rule violators to teaching prosocial values of mutual respect create more manageable educational climates.[45]

- **Demanding greatness instead of obedience:**[46] Many assume that the choice in management philosophy is between obedience or permissiveness. There is another option that is neither authoritarian nor permissive. This is to demand mature, responsible behavior. It is not acceptable for youth to run roughshod over the rights of others. Adults must challenge hurting behavior and hold children accountable, but in ways that call forth the great potential of young people. For clarity, these examples contrast demanding obedience versus demanding greatness.

  - "Bullying the new student in our class violates school rules, so you are going to be punished."

  - "I know you want to be respected, and that is the way you are expected to treat others in our class."

- **Reversing responsibility:** Maturity requires taking responsibility for one's failures and weaknesses. Instead, many rationalize, deny, project, or excuse—anything to avoid acknowledging that one has been wrong. Dodging responsibility becomes a high art form with youth who blame others for their difficulties. But taking ownership of problems is the first step in resolving them. Thus, a person who *puts off responsibility* can be countered by an adult or peer who *reverses responsibility*. Here are examples.

  - A student seeks to excuse poor school attendance by telling a counselor, "Well, my parents are alcoholics, so what do you expect?" The counselor reverses this by saying simply, "Then I guess it's up to you."

- When a drug-abusing youth rationalizes that "Lots of adults use drugs of some kind, too," peers in a counseling group retort, "How does that give you a right to hurt yourself?"

- A youth who reacts to the slightest affront with aggression and brags that "Nobody messes with me" is challenged to have enough self-confidence that "Nobody's words can make you feel small."

The goal is not to attack a person but to communicate a belief in the young person's ability to take charge of his or her life. We recall a youth in a peer-helping group explaining the ropes to a newcomer: "They even talk to you different here. Whatever you say, it's like they hold up a mirror and you find the answer somewhere inside of yourself."

Coping and Conflict Cycles

Nicholas J. Long pioneered the conflict cycle model to teach adults and youth how to resolve conflict.[47] Youth who present problems can easily lure adults into unhelpful conflicts. In a type of *reverse behavior modification*, the adult mirrors a youth's maladaptive behavior. Dealing with an angry person makes us angry, and dealing with someone who is depressed makes us feel depressed. Further, a child who distrusts adults may respond with hostility or avoidance, even to friendly overtures.

Why is it easier for an aggressive youth to get a caring professional to act crazy than it is for a caring professional to get a disturbed youth to act normal?

—Nicholas J. Long[48]

Figure 6.1 shows our elaboration of this model, the CLEAR Coping and Conflict Cycle. In table 6.3, we use the acronym *CLEAR* to describe this brain-based problem-solving process and provide a classroom example of it in action.

Child psychiatrist Susan J. Bradley of the University of Toronto sees the failure to regulate emotional arousal as the prime cause of psychopathology.[49] Coercive interventions heighten physical, emotional, and social stress.

To avoid this escalating conflict involves controlling inner emotions and external challenges. Calming oneself as well as the other person defuses conflict. These are coping skills that both staff and youth can learn to apply to all their human relationships. The challenge is to turn a self-defeating conflict cycle into an adaptive

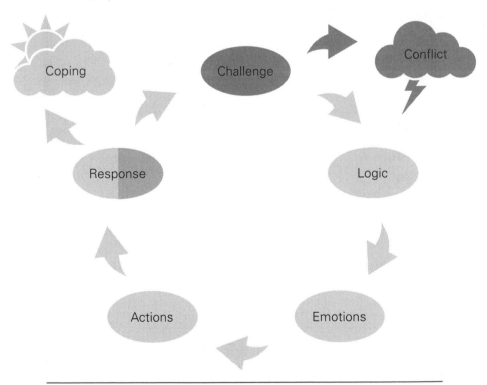

Figure 6.1: CLEAR Coping and Conflict Cycle.

Table 6.3: CLEAR Problem-Solving Sequence and Example

CLEAR	The Brain's Problem-Solving Sequence	An Example of Classroom Conflict
Challenge	A stressful event registers in the brain's amygdala.	A teacher publicly criticizes a student.
Logic	The logical brain evaluates the challenge.	The student thinks, "She is disrespecting me."
Emotions	The brain triggers emotions to motivate action.	The student becomes angry at the teacher.
Actions	Behavior occurs based on logic and emotions.	The student insults the teacher.
Response	Others' reactions lead to coping or conflict.	The teacher reacts to the provocation. • **Coping:** If the adult responds with calmness and empathy, the student is soothed and supported. The conflict ends, and the youth's ability to cope is strengthened. • **Conflict:** If the adult mirrors an angry student, conflict escalates and what might have been a small problem can become a crisis. Everyone loses.

coping cycle. Here are five strategies educators and youth practitioners can use for this purpose.

1. **Defuse the youth's agitation:** Be attuned to signs of emotional arousal in facial expression and tone of voice; try to understand what a youth is feeling and saying.

2. **De-escalate your own arousal:** This requires awareness of inner cues of your anger, fear, or disgust. Self-calm or disengage until you are no longer telegraphing rancor.

3. **Allow time for cooling down:** Intense emotions naturally fade, so time is our ally. A calm and concerned tone of voice and demeanor can often quiet turbulent emotions.

4. **Never take anger personally:** We do not want to add more pain to a student already in pain. When empathy replaces blame, we are motivated to tend and befriend.[50]

5. **Model a generous spirit:** Small acts of kindness can have restorative effects, and showing forgiveness provides a model of how to restore ruptured relationships.

When we approach the coping and conflict cycle in this way, challenges and conflict become problems to solve.

Developing Resilient Problem Solving

The brain is equipped to solve challenging problems and to take pleasure in solutions. Because humans have a highly developed social brain, we rely heavily on one another to help us cope successfully and overcome difficulty. We develop resilience through relational support. The brain's natural helping process follows three steps of *connect*, *clarify*, and *restore*.[51]

1. **Connect:** One way to solve problems is to go solo, reflect on the situation, and seek solutions. If this doesn't work, we get snared in worry and rumination. Another option is to seek out a trusted person.[52] By connecting, we gain emotional encouragement and help from another in solving the problem.

2. **Clarify:** The brain is designed to make sense of life events. We do this by constructing stories based on timelines of

key events, thus gaining insight into ourselves and our world. This process follows the brain-based sequence we call *CLEAR*. We describe this further in the next section.

3. **Restore:** Once we understand the nature of a problem, we are better able to find solutions that restore inner and interpersonal harmony. Problems come from unmet needs. Life is in balance when we feel safe and meet basic needs.

All thinking starts with "felt difficulty."... A solution leads to the "development of delight."

—*John Dewey*[53]

To distill this chapter's discussion into a few guiding principles, the following reclaiming strategies summarize the road to resilience.

Connect:

- **Safety:** Build trust to calm and engage a person in conflict.
- **Empathy:** Respond to needs instead of reacting to problems.

Clarify:

- **Communication:** Explore key life events to identify coping styles.
- **Insight:** Reframe problems as opportunities for learning.

Restore:

- **Supports:** Provide relationships that promote resilience.
- **Strengths:** Foster Belonging, Mastery, Independence, Generosity.

In the following three sections, we elaborate on the mechanisms underlying CLEAR thinking, we examine CLEAR as a timeline of events in the mind of a youth under duress, and we explore how teams can use CLEAR to identify problems and develop support systems for students.

CLEAR Thinking

In this section, we identify practical strategies for communicating with youth in conflict. Building on our earlier discussion of the CLEAR model, the following explores in greater depth how the brain manages conflict.

- **Challenge:** A stressful event triggers the amygdala. This is the brain's security system which spots danger or opportunity. In a fraction of a second, the amygdala signals the logical and emotional brain to find an appropriate response.[54]

- **Logic:** The *reasoning brain* evaluates the event. This area of the brain analyzes incoming stimuli in order to clarify the nature of the stressor. If it perceives safety, the higher brain shuts down the stress reaction systems.

- **Emotions:** The *emotional brain* motivates action. Beyond fear and rage, mammals have emotional brain circuits for social bonding, exploring, play, and caring.[55] Humans also have emotions based on sense of self, such as pride and shame.

- **Actions:** *Coping behavior* serves to restore balance. Coping behavior is designed to deal with internal and external stressors. This includes purposeful behavior as well as unconscious emotional reactions like defense mechanisms.

- **Response:** *Consequences* of actions impact self and others. Actions have positive or negative results—both overt or hidden. Particularly important are how individuals interpret actions and how these evoke reactions from others.

In the following two sections, we examine CLEAR as a timeline of events in the mind of a youth under duress, and we explore how teams can use CLEAR to identify problems and develop support systems for students.

CLEAR Timeline of Events

In any behavioral incident, the brain copes with challenges using the CLEAR problem-solving process. To understand a crisis with a youth, you must jointly construct a timeline of the event. Figure 6.2 illustrates this sequence.

CLEAR Timeline
The Brain's Natural Problem-Solving Process

Challenge	Logic	Emotions	Action	Response
What triggered the event?	What was the person thinking?	What was the person feeling?	What was the specific behavior?	What was the final outcome?

Figure 6.2: The CLEAR timeline.

In CLEAR problem solving, we get the timeline of an event in a natural conversation, and we can use that timeline to assess how a person copes with challenge. Instead, mentor and youth reconstruct the timeline of an event to clarify what happened. This is a way to understand the causes (function and purpose) of behavior. Young people are able to learn how problems arise and how their behavior affects the self and others.

Schools use the simple visual format of a youth on a timeline to replace consequence-bound behavior incident reports. Although the adult may choose to ask questions, such as those listed beneath the timeline, the student version does not include the explanatory text shown in figure 6.2. Student and adult complete a timeline around some incident, such as getting kicked out of class.

Although one can simply draw a horizontal arrow on a piece of paper, we find that students get engaged with a simple diagram showing an action figure on a horizontal arrow.

A simple example might be a natural conversation between an adult and a student that is able to establish the following.

- **Challenge:** The student is stressed about being bullied.
- **Logic:** The student thinks he has no friends who will stand up for him.
- **Emotions:** The student is feeling angry and depressed.
- **Action:** The student has been attempting to cope by skipping school.
- **Response:** Truancy is only adding the problem of school failure.

In discussions with the student, the adult jots notes about the sequence of the event on top of the line. Then, the student can express inner logic and feelings beneath the line. Some students ask to keep their timelines, and staff use these data for reports.

The use of a timeline to understand behavior is not new. Many schools use a timeline called *ABC*, which stands for *antecedents*, *behavior*, and *consequence*. In simple terms, behavior results from events that precede and follow it. Despite its wide use, the ABC timeline omits crucial information about behavior—inner thoughts and feelings. The CLEAR timeline better matches how the brain really works.

CLEAR Teamwork

In addition to providing youth with timelines to understand their own feelings and thoughts, professionals and parents need easily understood systems to identify problems and develop support systems for students. Adults can use the CLEAR format as an agenda for organizing brief team meetings to gather information to support youth in conflict.[56] Students and parents have important information to contribute to this discussion.

The meeting begins by listing the strengths of the young person. Then, the team sets up columns on a whiteboard to collect information on each of the CLEAR metrics, such as the following.

- **Challenges:** List stressors facing the student.
- **Logic:** Note how the student interprets these challenges.
- **Emotions:** Identify the student's feelings and goals.
- **Actions:** Focus on key behavioral concerns.
- **Response:** Review resulting consequences.

Once the nature of the problem is clarified, participants can seek restorative solutions by providing external supports and building internal strengths based on the Circle of Courage.

In conclusion, our mentor William Morse warns against preoccupation with techniques and strategies.[57] We guide youth on the pathways to responsibility by building relationships that enable young people to thrive.

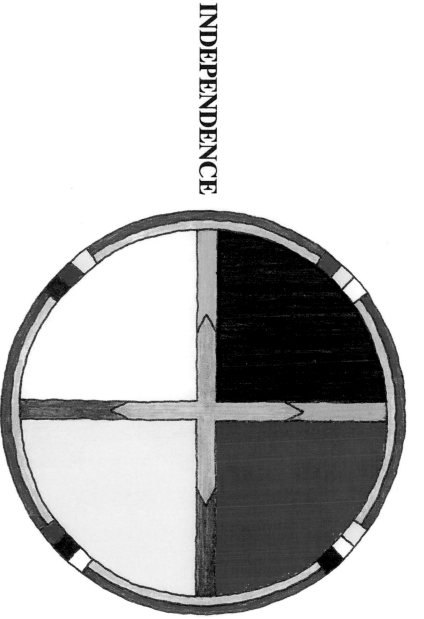

INDEPENDENCE

GENEROSITY

MASTERY

BELONGING

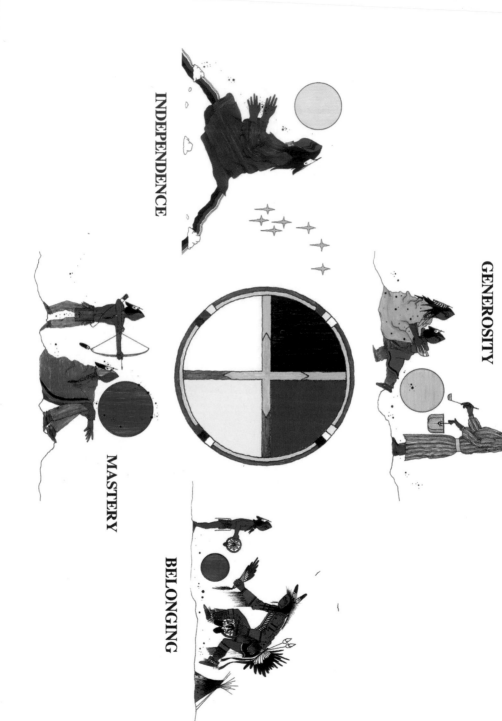

INDEPENDENCE

GENEROSITY

MASTERY

BELONGING

BELONGING

MASTERY

GENEROSITY

CHAPTER 7

Lives With Purpose: Strengthening Altruism

Only a positive prosocial purpose can provide the lasting inspiration, motivation, and resilience that is characteristic of a truly purposeful life.

—*William Damon*[1]

For 99 percent of human evolution, people lived in hunter-gatherer groups. Thus, our genetic code equips us to thrive in cultures of cooperation.[2] Many attribute the phrase *survival of the fittest* to Charles Darwin, but it was philosopher Herbert Spencer who first coined it.[3] That this became the battle cry for Social Darwinism to justify war, racism, and subjugation of women is deeply tragic.

Contrary to the *everyone for themselves* myth, Charles Darwin believed that compassion was the strongest instinct in humans.[4] He became absorbed in studying concern for others—which he called *sympathy*—after the death of his beloved young daughter. He concluded that compassion was even stronger than self-interest in most persons and noted that "those communities which included the greatest number of the most sympathetic members would flourish the best."[5]

Throughout history, successful educators shared a common vision of the great potential of youth. In the first book on adolescence published in 1904, G. Stanley Hall describes this stage as a second birth, marked by a rise of moral idealism.[6] Writing in 1909, Jane Addams picked up on this concept in proposing the antidote to rampant materialism is to tap the "wonderful and inexplicable instinct for justice" of youth.[7]

Johann H. Pestalozzi penned the classic account of the eagerness of children to help others. Here he describes his conversation with his orphans at Stans, Switzerland, upon hearing that a fire had destroyed a neighboring village:

> I gathered the children round me, and said, "Altdorf has been burnt down; perhaps, at this very moment, there are a hundred children there without home, food, or clothes; will you not ask our good Government to let twenty of them come and live with us?"
>
> I still seem to see the emotion with which they answered, "Oh, yes, yes!" "But, my children," I said, "think well of what you are asking! Even now we have scarcely money enough, and it is not at all certain that if these poor children come to us, the Government would give us any more than they do at present, so that you might have to work harder, and share your clothes with these children, and sometimes perhaps go without food. Do not say, then, that you would like them to come unless you are quite prepared for all these consequences."
>
> But they were not in the least shaken in their decision, and all repeated, "Yes, yes, we are quite ready to work harder, eat less, and share our clothes, for we want them to come."[8]

There has been a long history of debate about altruism in philosophy and psychology.[9] Among the Roman elite, it was an obligation to establish one's nobility with extravagant displays of charity to those of inferior birth (*noblesse oblige*). To the sociobiologist, helping behavior may result from an instinctual drive to protect related members of one's species. Many psychological theorists suggest that selfishness lurks beneath seemingly selfless acts of generosity.[10] Thus, a person joins a service club to make business contacts. But it is empathy with another person that evokes genuine altruism.

Empathy involves both the emotional and logical brain.[11] From birth, children have the capacity for emotional empathy, although other factors, such as autism, can impact this. By school age, they gain the ability to understand what others may be thinking. This mind-reading ability is called *theory of mind*.[12] Empathy motivates helping behavior aimed at meeting the other person's needs. While genuine altruism may yield rewards, these are not the goals of helping.

Psychologist John C. Gibbs of The Ohio State University describes *respect* based on empathy as the highest level of moral development.[13] Figure 7.1 shows this.

At the bottom of the ladder is *power*, the belief that might makes right. The next step, *deals*, involves behavior driven by reward and punishment. Most humans advance to *cooperation* where they seek to get along with others, even without externally imposed consequences. This enables persons to function in social groups, but they may go along with group behavior that violates outsiders. The highest level of moral development is *respect*, acting with concern for others. Grounded in the spirit of Generosity, this is the goal for all our children.

A Curriculum for Caring

Urie Bronfenbrenner calls for a *curriculum for caring* as an antidote to self-centered lifestyles that are common in modern culture.[14]

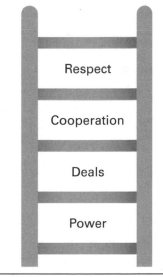

Figure 7.1: Levels of moral development.

Respect

Cooperation

Deals

Power

He writes that young people have few opportunities to contribute to the betterment of their families, friends, schools, and communities:

> It is now possible for a young person 18 years of age to graduate from an American high school without ever having had to do a piece of work on which someone else depended. Equally disastrous from this same perspective, it is possible for a young person, female as well as male, to graduate from high school, college, or university without ever having held a baby in his or her arms for longer than a few seconds, without ever having had to comfort or assist another human being who really needed help.[15]

One should not assume that the blame lies with the young people. They reflect values of societal institutions where some succeed at the expense of others.

The purpose for a curriculum for caring is not to learn *about* caring; instead, it asks youth to spend time caring for others. This includes elders, younger children, the sick, and the lonely. Such service activities are not restricted to the school but can be carried out in the greater community.

Kurt Hahn, the founder of Outward Bound, was a strong advocate of educational activities to teach compassion. He believed that youth desperately needed to contribute to a cause beyond themselves, to find some *grande passion*. He noted that there were three ways to motivate such service, namely, persuasion, compulsion, and attraction: "You can preach at them: that is a hook without a worm; You can order them to volunteer: that is dishonest; You can call on them: you are needed, and that approach will hardly ever fail."[16]

Research documents many positive results of volunteer service including increased responsibility, moral development, and commitment to democratic values.[17] Although these are laudable goals, many educators are skeptical that such programs may interfere with the school's busy agenda of academic learning. But intellectual gains can accrue from service-learning.[18] These include:

- Motivating students who are bored with school by linking academic learning with real human needs

- Increasing achievement of students who work as volunteer peer tutors

- Increasing students' problem-solving abilities

- Developing more complex thinking patterns

Perhaps the most powerful impact of helping others is that it shifts the focus from one's own problems to the needs of others. The pioneer of stress psychology was Hungarian-Canadian researcher Hans Selye, who mapped the biology of the body's HPA stress reaction system. Selye considered altruism as the ultimate resource for coping with life's stressors, for in helping another, one breaks free from preoccupation with the self.[19] Neuroscience shows that humans are exquisitely designed for caring and cooperative behavior, which has ensured our survival as a species.[20]

Young people can only develop a sense of self-worth by contributing to others. A central goal of peer-helping programs is to teach caring values and behavior to young people who have otherwise distinguished themselves by self-centered, antisocial lifestyles.[21] Here are some examples of successful service-learning projects from our own experience.

- Youth from an alternative school for students at risk assisted in the Special Olympics and went on camping trips with students who were blind.

- Elementary students bought groceries for needy families using money that would have been spent on repairing vandalism to their school.

- Youngsters prepared a home for a refugee family, planting flowers and bringing toys to welcome the children.

- Teenagers chopped firewood for the disabled, visited senior citizens, and organized a clown show for a day-care center.

There is rich practice wisdom on how to organize and operate such activities in schools and youth agencies.[22] The most successful projects are exciting and spontaneous rather than regimented or highly adult directed. There is usually a balance between short-term projects and those requiring long-term commitments. Activities that involve direct people-to-people contact usually have greater learning value than more indirect service. Projects that appeal to the strength of young people (such as, "This will be a tough job.") bring greater satisfaction than those that are less challenging. It is always important to involve the young people in developing, executing, and evaluating the projects.

The most difficult challenge in getting youth at risk to commit to a curriculum of caring often lies in the idea that service work is a waste of time or is otherwise uncool. We counteract these by making the act of caring fashionable and tap into each youth's spirit of adventure.

Making Caring Fashionable

Rebellious and rule-breaking behavior brings more status in some groups than does caring. In his pioneering book on reclaiming youth, Samuel R. Slavson notes that "the boys viewed their destructive, antisocial, and often brutal acts with surface calm and recounted them with bravado."[23] The challenge is to instill prosocial values that tap the brain-based spirit of generosity, which is stifled in many youth.[24] Youth sometimes glamorize problem behavior with terms that mask the real nature of the underlying values.

Youth who glorify destructive behavior do not view caring as cool. Helpful, sensitive, and prosocial actions get labels such as *sissy, narc,* or *brown-noser*. Urban graffiti proclaim that *snitches get stitches*. This Newspeak is toxic precisely because cultures reinforce core values with language. When hurting is rationalized, and helping is ridiculed, propaganda rules.

Unless moral deception is unmasked, young people are indoctrinated into antisocial values and lifestyles. Although adults can have a positive effect by the quiet, caring model they present, direct verbal intervention may be necessary to call out hurting behavior. This uses the verbal strategy of *relabeling* behavior. If hurting or immature acts are cast as clever or cool, these can be relabeled in simple, real-time sound bites. Consider the following examples.

- A macho street idiom for theft is *rip-off.* You can relabel this macho-sounding term in a diminutive way as *being sneaky*.
- Challenge the youth who bullies a younger child to show *I'm the boss* as *acting immature*.

In contrast, promote helping behavior with accurate labels such as *strong, courageous, intelligent,* or *attractive*. Label destructive acts more accurately with pejorative terms like *weak* or *foolish*. Never attach such negative labels to the young person, only to the behavior. For this approach to be effective, the adult must succeed in conveying the genuine message that this is irresponsible behavior for such a great young person.

Tapping the Spirit of Adventure

Many of the difficulties of youth are related to the fact that they are highly spirited and adventurous. A distinctive feature of youthful misbehavior is the celebration of prowess. Such youth are not motivated by the humdrum of typical schools. Their search for fun and adventure often leads to excitement through risk-seeking behavior. The spectacle of youth gangs has this quality. With the code of the warrior, they defend their turf and honor, turning aggression and toughness into virtues.

The challenge then becomes to redefine what courage is, such as through wilderness adventure programs, which are rich with courage-building activities.[25] When struggling against the elements, it is not just adults demanding greatness, but the challenge of survival itself. Even the most resistant youth has no need to defy the law of natural consequences. Such activities provide a powerful learning experience for youth that traditional methods do not easily reach.

Kurt Hahn believed the foremost task of education is to build values of courage and responsibility. Adults do not impose these values on youth but instead create powerful educational experiences that spontaneously call forth the capacity within them: "I regard it as the foremost task of education to ensure the survival of these qualities: an enterprising curiosity, an indefatigable spirit, tenacity in pursuit, readiness for sensible self-denial, and above all, compassion."[26]

Positive Relational Support

Canadian resilience researcher Kiaras Gharabaghi contends that most so-called evidence-based interventions ignore the power of relational child and youth care. Control of behavior is still the dominant mindset in education and youth work.[27] Many professionals are looking for ways to make youth less troublesome. The formula is simple—reward good behavior, punish bad behavior, and exclude those who fail to comply.

Three current approaches to manage behavior have vied for superiority: zero tolerance, positive behavior support (PBS), and social-emotional learning (SEL).[28] Presumably, we can immediately cast aside zero tolerance, since it fails to improve either school safety or student behavior.[29] In contrast, both PBS and SEL have their own extensive evidence base but differ in philosophy and strategies.

- **Positive behavior support:** This approach, which some refer to as *positive behavioral interventions and support*

(PBIS), has roots in behaviorism. Federal funding in special education promotes PBS as a blueprint for schools.[30] Although PBS emphasizes positive reinforcement over punishment, behavioral theory is still tied to extrinsic reinforcers.[31] However, the PBIS website (www.pbis.org) endorses holistic goals of promoting social, emotional, and academic outcomes.

- **Social-emotional learning:** This approach, which is promoted by the Collaborative for Academic, Social, and Emotional Learning (https://casel.org), draws from research in developmental psychology and resilience.[32] Where PBS is largely *adult directed*, SEL seeks to build *self-discipline* as students engage in prosocial behavior under their own volition.[33] An extensive meta-analysis of school-based SEL programs shows significant gains in social and emotional skills, attitudes, behavior, and academic performance.[34] Consistent with the Circle of Courage, SEL seeks to strengthen relationships, learning, responsibility, and empathy.

Both PBS and SEL promote positive behavior and avoid exclusionary punishment, but they differ in philosophy and strategies. PBS emphasizes *demandingness* with clear behavior expectations, rules, and consequences. SEL seeks *responsiveness* through positive relationships. George G. Bear, Sara A. Whitcomb, Maurice J. Elias, and Jessica C. Blank consider a major criticism of PBS to be its focus on behavioral control, while SEL has lacked specific methods to manage problems.[35] Reclaiming strategies are designed to address both relational and behavioral management goals.

In the remainder of this section, we examine school adoption of positive relational-support practices and how schools can adopt a tiered intervention system for providing support to youth at risk.

The Primacy of Relational Support

Although educators have used PBS and SEL as part of formal instruction, this practice has met resistance. Adding emotional and behavioral lessons to the crowded curriculum can compete with academic goals. Yet the most powerful interventions are relationship based.[36] Thus, the most promising approaches are not pedagogical but build a positive climate. David Osher and Juliet Berg provide an online resource reviewing approaches that have positive impact on school climate and socioemotional competence.[37] Natural relationships in a culture of caring foster growth and learning without changing the curriculum.[38]

Unfortunately, widespread adoption of PBS and SEL practices remains an ongoing challenge. An expert in education, parenting, and human behavior, Alfie Kohn challenges a wide range of school reforms as fads and distractions from what matters most.[39] He takes aim at both punishments and rewards in his book, *Punished by Rewards: The Trouble With Gold Stars, Incentive Plans, A's, Praise, and Other Bribes*.[40] He contends that hyperindividualism and cutthroat competition pit students against one another in the struggle for educational fitness.

Neuroscience shows that the brain itself has evolved to operate best in caring communities. For one hundred thousand years, humans lived in harmony in small bands of closely related people. As psychologist Louis Cozolino states, "We can enhance education by stimulating the social and emotional elements of the groups in which brains evolved to learn."[41]

Research on social and emotional learning has sparked interest in building caring schools.[42]

School Intervention Practices

Schools face a myriad of competing goals, including the race to raise test scores. In the process, basic needs can be ignored. In *Schools*

That Matter, Steve Van Bockern describes strategies educators are using to meet universal growth needs hardwired into the brain at birth.[43] The book proposes shifting the emphasis from standardized test data to ensuring schools meet the needs of all students.

To this end, educators need a system to match interventions with needs—sometimes called response to intervention (RTI). This model originated in public health but is seeing growing adoption in education. Intervention practices are categorized into a three-tiered system represented as an inverted pyramid. From the book *Taking Action*, figure 7.2 shows the three levels of this pyramid as applied to school and team responsibilities for educators.[44]

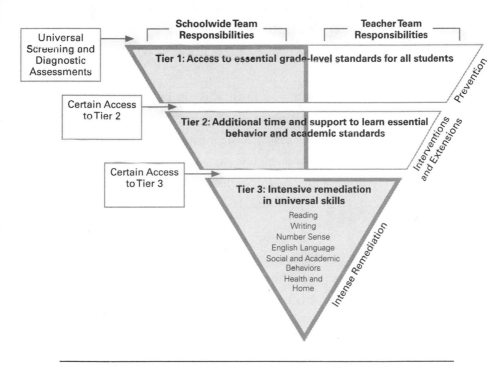

Figure 7.2: Tiers of intervention for educators.[45]

The following list highlights some key aspects of these support levels and how we view them within the context of Circle of Courage values.

- **Tier 1 (prevention):** This tier is preventative in nature and involves ensuring *all* students meet essential standards related to a school's core instruction. We believe that success in this tier requires creating a positive climate that meets the needs of both adults and students, based on biosocial needs and Circle of Courage values.

- **Tier 2 (interventions and extensions):** This tier focuses on those students who require additional time and relational support to address behavioral issues or reach Tier 1 academic standards. To have success at this tier, schools and youth-serving organizations need to have concrete methods to intervene and succeed with students facing personal or academic struggles. The CLEAR framework we outlined in chapter 6 (page 85) is an example of this kind of intervention.

- **Tier 3 (intense remediation):** This tier indicates a need for intense remediation to better connect with and support those students with the most serious and complex behavioral issues or academic support needs. Students with serious or chronic problems require a reclaiming plan based on an individualized, trauma-informed assessment of strengths and needs.

Planning Restorative Outcomes details a strength-based model of assessment for intervention built on Circle of Courage principles (also see https://reclaimingyouthatrisk.org).[46] Because research shows that developmental relationships are the active ingredient of successful interventions with youth,[47] we think it is important to view interventions through the lens of positive *relational* support as opposed to positive *behavior* support. Such support points to the need for having a culture of respect.

A Culture of Respect

There has been a persistent myth that youth at risk are likely to have negative influence on one another—stated in deficit-mindset terms as *deviant peer influence.*[48] Seen in this light, programs that bring together groups of such young people are described as *iatrogenic* which means the treatment makes the problem worse. One significant, and far more helpful, rediscovery in modern research has been to see the power of peers as an asset, not a liability.[49]

Persons who have encountered adverse life experiences have much to contribute to others. Many young people at risk can be more effective helpers than trained professionals, and there are creative strategies for engaging youth in helping one another. When we described this peer empowerment philosophy to a prominent psychiatrist, his response was that it is dangerous to give responsibility to irresponsible youth. We would counter that this kind of thinking represents the antithesis of a curriculum for caring and that the real danger lies in such attitudes that keep young people from full participation in our schools and communities.

It seems unreasonable to expect that a group of youth with behavior problems will somehow generate prosocial values and group norms.

—Scott W. Henggeler, Sonja K. Schoenwald, Charles M. Borduin, Melisa D. Rowland, and Phillippe B. Cunningham[50]

A wide range of innovative youth-empowerment programs have been established in regular and alternative schools and treatment settings. Decades of research document the efficacy of peer-helping groups. A prominent example is Positive Peer Culture (PPC), pioneered at Starr Commonwealth.[51] PPC has been researched and refined and is listed as an evidence-based intervention.[52] The central thesis is the belief that even troubled individuals have strengths and potential. Rather than focusing solely on stopping problem behavior, young people are empowered to help one another and make responsible decisions.[53] The goal is to tap these resources by enlisting young people in helping their peers.[54]

Positive staff teams are a prerequisite to positive youth cultures.[55] For information about PPC training, visit our website (https:// reclaimingyouthatrisk.org). Youth and staff collaborate to solve problems and meet Circle of Courage needs. You can see this effect in an account of young people involved in the peer-helping process.

At a professional conference in Germany, we met a group of youth who were alive with purpose and hope. These teens led a workshop where they described the core values they had chosen to guide their relationships with peers and adults:

> We treat each other with respect!
> We look out for one another!
> We help others if they have problems!
> We reject all physical or psychological violence![56]

Such values challenge the self-centered mindset common in society. These young people boldly espoused democratic principles of treating all persons with dignity. Most were immigrants to Germany whose own experience with violence had shown that only values of respect can counter abuse of power.

So how did these youth create their culture of respect? They are part of a PPC program in a unit of a large young-offender prison near Adelsheim in southern Germany. Accompanying them to their conference presentation was a veteran prison guard. He recounted that many correctional staff used to call in sick because of the stress of this job. "But now we enjoy coming to work!" he exclaimed. Although confined in a secure prison, these youth have formed bonds of respect with their peers and adults in authority.

We had first visited Adelsheim two years earlier as PPC Germany launched this peer-helping program in a secure unit of a sprawling prison. We explained to the two dozen teens that they would be asked to help one another. The goal was to encourage each young person to develop strengths in the four areas of the Circle of Courage. We brought copies of color drawings portraying these concepts. The youth were intrigued that Native American artist George Blue Bird could share his own experience of being incarcerated.

While wary of typical flaw-fixing treatment, the youth quickly embraced the four positive goals of Belonging, Mastery, Independence, and Generosity. It is little surprise that young people seek to belong, for such is the lure of gangs. Further, they want to succeed, even though they may struggle in school; and, seeking independence and power is a centerpiece of adolescence. But many who assume humans are self-centered overlook generosity—getting teens hooked on helping.[57]

Recounting their transformation of values to professionals in their workshop, one youth observed, "We used to have fights every day, but now we never fight because we have learned to treat one another as human beings." This is particularly noteworthy since they had widely diverse ethnic backgrounds.

When PPC groups mix with residents of other prison units, the contrast is dramatic. Those not involved in peer helping feel they must put on a front of toughness and sometimes ridicule PPC youth as being soft. But these young people are secure in their core values: "We treat each other with respect."

There is a growing body of evidence that programs of peer involvement not only neutralize anti-authority behavior, but also create positive learning climates that foster social and academic development.[58] The benefits include enhanced self-esteem, increased internal locus of control, increased prosocial values, and reversal of long-standing patterns of school failure and underachievement.

Young people are not just future leaders—they have great untapped potential for responsible leadership. In a world of chaos and conflict, we find wisdom in the words of young people from the Adelsheim Prison: "Violence in any form includes humiliation and depreciation of the other person. When we engage in violence, we want to make the other 'small' and ourselves superior. That stands in bold contrast to showing respect to one another."[59]

Enduring Wisdom

The values of the Circle of Courage we outline in chapters 4–7 are demonstrated in the actions of those who emerged at many times in history to bring dignity to the lives of children. Sometimes these were tribal persons who nurtured the sacred fires in cultures where caring for the young was the core value. Throughout much of Western civilization, they were prophetic voices calling for a restoration of dignity to children of discouragement.

Educational approaches in Europe were influenced by pioneers such as Johann Pestalozzi and Maria Montessori.[60] In the United States, Horace Mann championed schooling for all and challenged students at Antioch College to be ashamed to die until they had won some great victory for humanity.[61]

Truths which were once new must be constantly renewed by being pronounced again from the depths of the ardent personal convictions of a new human being.

—Ellen Key[62]

The 20th century opened with a spirit of great optimism but was to end without fulfilling its destiny as *the century of the child*. The life of Janusz Korczak of Poland, a champion of the child's right to respect, portrays the heights and the depths of this era.[63] He was revered as an author and director of a school and orphanage for

Jewish street children. When Nazis occupied Poland, they confined the orphans and staff to the Warsaw ghetto.

Knowing they soon would be sent to a death camp, Korczak prepared them for what was to come. The children produced a play based on Rabindranath Tagore's *Post Office*, the story of a dying Hindu boy. Then, on the day when the soldiers arrived, the children dressed in their best and paraded proudly beneath a green flag in the manner of *King Matt the First*. They proceeded to the railway station to board boxcars bound for the gas chambers of Treblinka. To avoid making Korczak a martyr, a Nazi officer offered him a Swiss passport for safe passage. "What kind of person would leave children at a time like this?" Korczak asked, choosing to remain with his staff and children.

Where that factory of death once stood, only the green of grass and trees surrounding a circle of stones remain. On the various rocks are inscribed the cities or countries from which one million people came to meet their end. The only individual name on any stone reads simply *Janusz Korczak and children*.

Following Korczak's death, friends recovered the manuscript for *Ghetto Diary* hidden behind a brick wall in the attic of the children's home. In his final entries, made in the summer of 1942, he wonders whether anyone in future generations will ever care about what he is writing, and then he sums up the meaning of his life in the words, "I exist not to be loved and admired, but to act and love."[64]

Across centuries and cultures, the saga of our forebears has been carried to us in this time and place. The responsibility is ours to keep that story alive. A society marked by alienation must rediscover its heritage of enduring values. Then, as Ellen Key said at the beginning of the 20th century, these truths will be renewed in the conviction of a new generation of human beings.[65] The responsibility for action and advocacy is in our hands.

CHAPTER 8

From Surviving to Thriving

Every trauma survivor I've met is resilient in his or her own way, and every one of their stories inspires awe at how people cope.

—*Bessel van der Kolk*[1]

We provide a capstone to this book with two powerful stories of the struggle to turn trauma into resilience. We begin with Emmy E. Werner, who chronicled the lives of children at risk born in 1955 on the Hawaiian Island of Kauai. Her preeminent studies spanned decades, forming the foundations of the field of resilience science.[2] As the children of Kauai reached fifty-five years of age, Larry K. Brendtro interviewed Werner about her research findings in light of the Circle of Courage. We present a condensed version of that interview here.[3]

In the final discussion, Martin Brokenleg shares perspectives on cultural trauma and resilience from his experience growing up on the Rosebud Lakota (Sioux) reservation. Martin's Lakota grandfather never spoke English and met his first Whiteman late in life. Martin's father, Noah, was stolen from his family as a small boy and sent to an Indian boarding school where he was punished if he spoke his Native tongue. While raised in two worlds, Noah Brokenleg was able to preserve and pass on his Native heritage to his children.

Risk, Resilience, and Recovery

By Emmy E. Werner

Interviewer: We want to draw on your insights from a half-century of research on risk and resilience.

Werner: My concern right now is the misuse of the concept of resiliency. Instead of brief accounts and cross-sectional studies, I think it is important to take a long-term perspective, because resilience is a process that takes time.

In the early years, Michael Rutter, Norman Garmezy, and I were independently discovering that not all so-called high-risk children turn out to be failures.[4] Garmezy came to this work through studying people with schizophrenia and their offspring.

Rutter has broad interests in anything that relates to risk and resilience. I think that of all who have studied adversity, he is probably the most insightful in terms of clarifying concepts. He is very remarkable and the only psychiatrist who has been knighted by the Queen of England. He is still very active and has done studies on Romanian adoptees and found a number of them who have done okay.[5]

Interviewer: Whether these children elicit positive or negative reactions is tremendously important in how they turned out in later life.

Werner: That is an important concept in turning things around. Through my work with UNICEF in India, Indonesia, and East Africa, I saw an awful lot of kids who were considered "high risk" but they seemed to be adapting amazingly well. Garmezy, Rutter, and I independently were beginning to wonder if this whole concept of risk was meaningful.

My own childhood was fairly risky in that my father was of French descent and my mother was German. Family members fought on different sides of the war. Every male member of my family died. I experienced five years of saturation bombing, and I still have a pretty good sense of humor. The point is that when in very risky situations, a lot of people do not think of this as being so unusual because there are all those other people on which bombs have been dropped.

The term *risk* began with the maritime insurance in 19th-century England when ships were being insured. Risk was a characteristic of the environment, or the ship, or the captain, that might lead to the loss of the ship or the success of the transaction. So let's say you are a captain who drinks a lot, you have a crew that isn't very happy with your schedule, and the ship is leaking—will you make it across? These are three high-risk factors. Your insurance rates would go up. Eventually the term was used in public health where it first referred to an *environmental risk*—but now children are called *high risk*. A *risk factor*, whether inside of you or outside, is a probability, not a certainty. But we treat risk in almost everything we write about as a certainty such as, "You are a child of two alcoholics, too bad."

Interviewer: Or, in the juvenile justice system, when a youth shows early conduct problems, many want to give up on him because this behavior predicts bad outcomes. A criminal adult most likely started in crime as a youth, but a youth who broke the law does not always continue breaking the law as an adult.

Werner: That is the key. If you look at it prospectively, you get a much more encouraging picture. Initially, Garmezy, Rutter, and I all thought something was wrong with our findings [of positive outcomes].

Researching Resilience

Werner: The initial study covered the first ten years. We looked back and saw the kids from poor homes with parents who hadn't graduated from high school, who were alcoholic, who had perinatal stress, and who had a lot of negative things happen to them—of course, we expected they would all turn out to have problems—at least by age eighteen. We began to see that this wasn't so. Many times, I questioned our statistics; we were so imbued with this idea that something had to be wrong. . . .

Interviewer: When did you see the concept of *resilience* come into use in our field? As I understand, the term began in physics. If an object is stressed, it can return to its original state.

Werner: One of my stepsons is an engineer and we were talking about this. That is when I first thought of it. These people may bend but don't break. . . . If you pick the main risk factors in children's lives, you have alcoholism, poverty (one out of five children), not being able to graduate from high school, premature birth, and early turbulence in the family. But then you see these kids in school who have no behavior problems, no learning problems, they have friends, they seem cheerful, they seem to attract peers; yes, you wonder, What is this?

We called our 1982 book *Vulnerable but Invincible: A Longitudinal Study of Resilient Children and Youth.* But in my opinion, the term *resilience* has been grossly misused. We have to keep clarifying that we cannot label a person as resilient; it is a process. Over time, young folks raised in adversity can adapt successfully to whatever demands are made of them. It is not that being resilient in the teen years means someone will be resilient at age one hundred, because there are changes. Most of the changes are in a positive direction.

I am glad we discovered what many already knew deep down— that adversity by itself does not need to destroy you. In fact, it can strengthen you and especially help you give back to others. What we are really talking about are individual differences in response to adversity, vulnerability, and resilience. . . .

At the fiftieth anniversary of the end of World War II in Europe, I was reviewing the evidence on what happened to kids who were bombed in Dresden, which was much worse than Hiroshima. Protective factors operated among those kids who had these horrible high-impact experiences. But there were physical problems that made it difficult in later life.

Post-traumatic stress disorder is another term that needs clarification. I should, myself, be totally stressed out having seen many, many piles of corpses. It is true that when the ambulance or police car passes by here, I still duck. But I think you have to differentiate between responses that you learn to survive and your capability of managing your life over time. . . .

The Circle of Courage and Resilience

Interviewer: The Circle of Courage resilience model focuses on Belonging, Mastery, Independence, and Generosity. Could you summarize the importance of these factors in your Hawaiian research? Let us begin with *Belonging* and *Attachment*.

Werner: I would say that is the key element. Even though children came from poor homes, if they had one adult who cared, this was consistently treasured by them. I saw it again in middle school, when they elicited relationships with special teachers, but also with one good friend who kept them going. I saw it again much later in middle age, when after maybe a dysfunctional first marriage, a second partner really accepted them, and they changed for the better. So, I think this is really the most basic thing on which you need to build everything else.

Interviewer: Years ago, Robert White said that competency motivation was one of the core human motives.[6] What did your research say about the importance of Mastery and Achievement?

Werner: Keep in mind that we are dealing with a population where more than half of the parents have not graduated from high school, where people generally are not—as wonderful as they are—as communicative as, say, middle-aged professors. But within that framework, I would say that Mastery became a very important motivator. It was not narrowly academic. This could be learning to help at home when someone else needed to work part time to provide food. Many would take care of younger siblings. It could be just showing off that you were good at hula. Competence, broadly based rather than just academic, was an important motivator. That continued in adulthood. Those who recovered from previous problems were often the ones who looked for higher education, adult education, or vocational education. Often, they joined the armed forces in order to get those skills, so, Mastery was a very important motivator.

Interviewer: Research shows the importance of self-efficacy and self-regulation.[7] So when you look at this dimension of *Independence* and *Autonomy*, what did your study say about that?

Werner: It was there and developed more strongly as they reached adolescence and young adulthood. It was linked together with a sense of required helpfulness. They were using their Autonomy not in selfish competition—"I'm going to get to Harvard if I have to trample on many toes"—but rather: "I am going to take care of myself because in this way I can help my sister who may be struggling with my parents' alcoholism." It was that sort of combination.

Interviewer: So, it was not "I am free to be my own person" but a sense of responsibility in partnership with others. This brings us to *Generosity* and *Altruism*. What do you see are the significant links to resilient outcomes?

Werner: Some sort of shared sense of faith was very predominant. The specific religion did not matter. There were Catholics and Buddhists (Buddhism is a major religion on Kauai). There were Mormons and Seventh-day Adventists. It was knowing that whatever they were doing, they were not alone, they were in a community. And it did not matter how often they went to church, but that somehow what they were doing had some meaning.

Emmy E. Werner (1929–2017) was professor at the University of California, Davis.

From Trauma to Resilience

By Martin Brokenleg

Resilience is closely intertwined with trauma. Dante Cicchetti and Kristin Valentino define it as "the capacity for adapting successfully and functioning competently, despite experiencing chronic stress or adversity following exposure to prolonged or severe trauma."[8] Indigenous populations worldwide are dealing with *intergenerational trauma* which is the result of colonization—the dominant culture sought to stamp out aboriginal ways. The ramifications of this are deep and far reaching.

The Legacy of Colonialization

Native American and First Nations cultures show the impact of cultural trauma of colonization. In *Dancing With a Ghost*, Rupert Ross describes complex post-traumatic stress disorder (PTSD).[9] His work in Canada documents the connection between colonialism and criminality. Both in my birthplace in South Dakota and my current home in British Columbia, Native people are over-represented in juvenile justice and corrections. Some might ask, "Is there something wrong with Native people?" The question is not What is wrong with Native people? but What has happened to them?

At first glance, colonization might seem like a positive process for harmonizing diverse populations. The United States has been described as a melting pot—presumably we should all become more alike. However, Canada has a philosophy rooted in multiculturalism—trying to maintain and respect differences in language, values, and traditions.

Colonization by the dominant culture was a central goal of school, church, and government. These social institutions gave a false interpretation about what has happened to us, why we are the way we are, and what we should become. However, in recent decades, Native communities began making a major shift. We are defining the world the way we see it, describing the dynamics as we understand them, and designing our own course for the future. We are telling our story.

Transmission of Trauma

Traumatic experiences are cumulative. If one generation does not heal, then later generations inherit those problems. This is both a transmission of cultural information as well as an epigenetic process.[10] Colonized groups, Holocaust survivors, and peoples who historically endured totalitarian societies may show these intergenerational effects of trauma.

In some form, this cultural trauma affects every Native person. It sculpts how we think and respond emotionally. It affects our social dynamics and, at the deepest level, our spirituality. Intergenerational trauma has wounded us deeply. There were times in my life that I wondered, "Is there something wrong with me?" and "What is wrong with us?" The truth is there is nothing wrong with Natives— we are normal people responding to an abnormal history.

Only by being aware of the deep dynamics of trauma have I found the means to cope. But approaches to trauma too often merely treat the symptoms. This may work with the flu or a cold when we take cough drops and aspirin. Educators and helping professionals dole out a lot of psychosocial aspirins.

For Native people, our deeper issue is related to intergenerational trauma. Whether intentional or not, trauma became the carrier for cultural genocide. I hesitate to use the word *genocide* because it is so potent, we can feel impotent. But this is what happened in my homeland, South Dakota, between 1860 and 1890. This was military genocide. My own grandfather told me stories about hiding from the U.S. Cavalry.

Canada did not experience this large-scale warfare. Intergenerational trauma was a government-enforced program of taking children away to residential schools. We have had a history of courts clogged with cases of abuses Native students suffered in these toxic settings. A person who experiences intergenerational trauma may shut down because grief is so great. Yet without recognizing a problem, it cannot be healed. Understanding how to heal from such trauma requires perspective on what it's like to live with it. This applies to traumatized persons worldwide, but I will focus on my experiences in North America.

Living With Trauma

What are the sources of trauma in Native life? Some have to do with dynamics that occurred in the past and are enshrined in formal federal and state policy. Most notable are the lifelong effects on children removed from their parents to be reared in boarding schools. I spoke with a woman in Winnipeg—a smartly dressed, articulate, intelligent teacher. When she was five years old, a plane landed in her community. The officials aboard took all the five-year-olds away, never to return home again. She does not know what happened to her parents or if she has brothers or sisters.

The power of the church was also deeply involved in this travesty. Notice I did not say Christianity or the teachings of Jesus, but the institutional church was complicit. The papal bull of 1493 authorized European princes to conquer and convert people from what they considered inferior Native cultures.[11] In North America, the doctrine of manifest destiny held that the United States was destined by God to occupy Native lands.[12] The church also played its part in the boarding school experience designed to eliminate Native culture.

Poverty hits Native people perhaps more than any other population, and poverty perpetuates trauma. For instance, lacking income to buy enough protein—peanut butter, meats, cheese, eggs—can impair a child's intelligence if the mother is malnourished during pregnancy. People living in poverty are vulnerable to other crises. Those with a decent income could probably miss a few days of work and make it through the month, but the poor cannot miss a half day of work and still put food on the table or pay their electrical bill. Poor populations are always at the mercy of the dynamics of life distress.

Various kinds of oppression create trauma. Sometimes this is deliberate, but most is imbedded in the institution. The under-representation of Native people in positions of power permeates corporate, educational, and governmental domains.

The worst kind of oppression is internalized. The first time I went to South Africa, I visited the grave of Steve Biko. He courageously fought for equality in apartheid South Africa but was killed in police custody. Biko often declared that "the most potent weapon in the hands of the oppressor is the mind of the oppressed."[13] If someone can convince us that we are not good enough, not smart enough, and not capable enough, then oppression becomes permanent in our minds.

Healing From Trauma

The Brazilian activist Paulo Freire declares that it is impossible for the oppressor to liberate the oppressed.[14] Thus, those of us who are suffering must do this work ourselves. I have been a professor for about forty years, and I had to find a way to talk about matters of the heart with those who were working with Native populations. One will never understand Native people by ignoring the spiritual dimension. Instead, we will meet resistance and hostility, overt or silent. Native cultures are intensely spiritual, the plane on which all the dynamics that matter occur.

Quite often, the youth gang becomes an artificial source of spirituality. It offers substitute sources of Belonging, which Indigenous communities once provided. We need to reclaim our traditional ways, even if only a few expressions in our Native language. In my Lakota tongue, the word for child is unlike the inferiority-nuanced English word. Instead, children are called *Wakan*, which literally means sacred. In reclaiming such expressions, we seek to recover the culture colonization stripped from us.

We see society-wide disregard of young people. One of the biggest threats among all youth is the absence of significant interpersonal relationships. Oddly, this is at a time when we "friend" on Facebook. We can twitter and tweet and cheep and chirp. What we really need are those face-to-face relationships that keep us strong.

Our schools are much better at dispensing facts than helping students flourish. *Knowledge* describes training of the mind, and we are in a mad race to do this with the goal of raising test scores. But there is another kind of learning which Aristotle called *capacities*.[15] We want to reach the heart. This is resiliency, being strong on the inside, having a courageous spirit. One cannot teach resiliency with words or posters—we need developmental relationships.

Belonging, Mastery, Independence, and Generosity are essential for healthy growth and for healing trauma. These values make up the Circle of Courage because resilience is the courage to surmount life challenge. Native psychologist Joseph Gone from Harvard observes that effective interventions for healing historic trauma will involve reclaiming traditional cultural knowledge.[16] This is a birthright for Indigenous children, and a bequest to all the children and youth of the world.

Relationships for Resilience

I end with a recollection from my youth. My parents were traditional Lakota people and seldom went anywhere without their children. The first time I was ever going to be away from my parents was when I was entering grade eleven. I do not recall where I got this idea, but I asked my parents if I could go to a boys' military school. They did not know anything about these places but said I should apply and see what happens. I applied to three military schools out east and was accepted at all three. I picked one, and that fall my parents drove me out with a carload of possessions. I had my new blue-grey uniforms. We had to buy our textbooks, so I had ordered boxes of these. We also had those round flat things called records, and I brought my collection and phonograph. I wore my uniform and marched around from September to December, and then it was home for the Christmas furlough back to the Rosebud reservation.

After wonderful holidays with my family, vacation came to an end. The winter weather was threatening, so my father decided it best that I fly back to school. As we drove toward Rapid City, the radio warned of a blizzard, predicting high winds, below zero temperatures, and tons of snow. My father left me at the downtown hotel in Rapid City as he hurried back to the reservation.

I arose early the next morning, and it was still dark. The snow was blowing sideways, and I could not even see the ground. I called the front desk and found that the shuttle was still scheduled for the 6 a.m. flight. I checked out of my room and sat down in the lobby near the window. Snow was blowing and, other than an occasional car, almost no one was on the streets.

The snow let up a bit, and I could see down the block. A shadow passed under the street light, and someone was leaning into the wind heading toward the hotel. The person came inside and shook the snow off her Pendleton blanket. I was surprised to see my father's cousin who lived a couple miles away. She had no car but had walked to see me before I departed.

She put her arms around me and said, "Son, I heard you were going back to school today, and I wanted to see you. How is your mother and how is your father?"

We sat down and talked until the shuttle bus pulled up. I stood up to go, and she put her arms around me again.

She said, "I want you to know that I am proud of you for staying in school. Someone in our family should have an education. You learn everything you can. I will think about you every day. I will pray for you every day."

She wrapped the blanket around herself and walked back out into the blowing snow. When someone cares for us amidst the blizzards of life, we know we belong.

Acknowledgments

Solution Tree Press would like to thank the following reviewers:

Casey Ahner
Principal
Tomé Elementary School
Los Lunas, Mew Mexico

Nancy Miles
Third-Grade Teacher
South Side Elementary School
Johnson City, Tennessee

Ryan Fuhrman
Seventh-Grade Science Teacher
Sheridan Junior High School
Sheridan, Wyoming

Rebecca Schnee
School Social Worker
Patrick Henry Elementary School
Colorado Springs, Colorado

Brian Kenney
Principal
Whittier Elementary School
Clinton, Iowa

Ashley Williams
Fifth-Grade Teacher
Sandhills Farm Life
    Elementary School
Carthage, North Carolina

Endnotes

About the Artist

[1] A full-color laminated Circle of Courage print is available from Starr Commonwealth (visit https://store.starr .org/Course/view/circle -of-courage-poster--- laminated-1).

[2] Whitney, 2015.

[3] Blue Bird, 2012.

Preface

[1] Chambers & Fraedo, 2015.

Introduction

[1] Slavson, 1965.

[2] Wolins & Wozner, 1982.

Chapter 1

[1] Wilson, 1998, p. 294.

[2] Wilson, 1998.

[3] Brendtro & Mitchell, 2015.

[4] Werry, 2013.

[5] Whewell, 1847.

[6] Wilson, 1998.

[7] As cited in Bertolino, 2014, p. 163.

[8] Boehm, 2012.

[9] Adler, 1985.

[10] Keller & Kärtner, 2013.

[11] Bolin, 2006.

[12] Korczak, 1967.

[13] Brendtro & Hinders, 1990.

[14] Modgil & Modgil, 2015.

[15] American Psychological Association Presidential Task Force on Evidence-Based Practice, 2006.

[16] Anglin & Brendtro, 2017.

[17] Einstein, 1954, p. 260.

[18] Brown & Seita, 2010; Hernandez, 2016.

[19] Vilakazi, 1993.

[20] Rogoff, 2003.

[21] Coolidge & Winn, 2018.

[22] Cajete, 2000.

[23] As cited in Brokenleg, 2014, p. 12.

[24] Shapin, 1998, p. 1.

[25] Keoke & Porterfield, 2002.

[76] Cross, 2012.

[27] Gone, 2015.

[28] Blumenkrantz, 2016.

[29] Mill, 2002.

[30] Maslow, 1959, p. 122.

[31] Brendtro & Mitchell, 2015.

[32] Li & Julian, 2012.

[33] Bronfenbrenner, 1979.

[34] Hanushek & Raymond, 2005.

[35] Luthar, 2006, p. 760.

[36] Jackson, 2014.

[37] Koltko-Rivera, 2006; Maslow, 1943.

[38] Coopersmith, 1967.

[39] Peter, 2000.

[40] Masten, 2014.

[41] Elias, Leverett, Duffell, Humphrey, Stepney, & Ferrito, 2015.

[42] Benard, 2004.

[43] Peterson, 2013.

[44] Kress, 2014; Lerner et al., 2013.

[45] Elliot, 2006.

[46] Freado, 2017.

[47] Bath & Seita, 2018.

[48] Strother, 2007.

[49] Ryan & Deci, 2017.

[50] Bolin, 2006, 2010.

[51] Common Ground, n.d.

Chapter 2

[1] Collier, 1947.

[2] Bird-David, 2017.

[3] Deloria, 2009.

[4] Hoffman, 1988.

[5] Erikson, 1963.

[6] Eastman, 2010.

[7] Gone, 2007.

[8] Reyhner & Eder, 2006.

[9] Densmore, 1929.

[10] Rogoff, 2003.

[11] A full-color laminated print is available from Starr Commonwealth (visit https://store.starr.org/Course/view/circle-of-courage-poster---laminated-1).

[12] Menninger, 1982.

[13] Deloria, 1998.

[14] Standing Bear, 2006, p. 7.

[15] Walker, 1982.

[16] Brokenleg & James, 2013.

[17] Deloria, 1998.

[18] Deloria & Wildcat, 2001.

[19] Eastman, 1911, p. 9.

[20] Pihama & Cameron, 2012.

[21] Brokenleg, 2010.

[22] Tam, Findlay, & Kohen, 2017.

[23] Gray, 2011, p. 140.

[24] As cited in Marty, 1987, p. 238.

[25] White, 1959.

[26] Standing Bear, 2006, p. 11.

[27] Kagan, 1971.

[28] Sylwester, 2005.

[29] Sternberg, 1996.

[30] Cajete, 2015.

[31] Standing Bear, 2006, p. 8.

[32] Deloria, 1998, p. 29.

[33] Standing Bear, 2006, p. 33.

[34] Johansen, 1998.

[35] Fisher & Frey, 2014.

[36] Eastman, 1919, p. 146.

[37] Standing Bear, 2006, p. 7.

[38] As cited in Hoffman, 1988, p. 116.

[39] Haines, 1888, p. 296.

[40] As cited in Hassrick, 1964, p. 316.

[41] Graff, 1987.

[42] Standing Bear, 2006, p. 19.

[43] Ryan & Deci, 2017.

[44] Maier, 1982.

[45] Bowlby, 1988.

[46] Hoffman, 2000.

[47] Perry & Szalavitz, 2010.

[48] Damon, 2008.

[49] E. Belleroe, personal communication, 1995.

[50] Densmore, 1929.

[51] Black Elk, 1932.

[52] Standing Bear, 2006.

[53] Eastman, 1902.

[54] Hassrick, 1964.

[55] Deloria, 1998.

[56] Bryde, 1971.

[57] Standing Bear, 2006, p. 15.

[58] Brendtro & Mitchell, 2015.

[59] Roehlkepartain & Scales, 2007.

[60] Callahan, 2010.

[61] Sneve, 1998, p. xii.

[62] Chambers & Freado, 2015.

[63] Maslow, 1959.

[64] Masten, 2014.

[65] Menninger, 1963.

[66] Collier, 1947, p. 12.

Chapter 3

[1] Cajete, 2012.

[2] Adler, 1930.

[3] Tillich, 1952.

[4] Anglin, 2002, p. 111.

[5] Hobbs, 1994.

[6] Gluckman & Hanson, 2006.

[7] James & Lunday, 2014.

[8] Bronfenbrenner, 1986.

[9] Sroufe, Egeland, Carlson, & Collins, 2005.

[10] Phelan, 2004.

[11] Bath & Seita, 2018; Tully & Brendtro, 1998.

[12] van der Kolk, 2014, p. 56.

[13] Obomsawin, Canell, & Verrall, 1987

[14] Tam, Findlay, & Kohen, 2017.

[15] Espiner & Guild, 2018.

[16] Greenwald, 2005, p. 37.

[17] Cozolino, 2014.

[18] Bryk, Sebring, Allensworth, Luppescu, & Easton, 2010.

[19] Turnbull, Turbiville, & Turnbull, 2000.

[20] McCall, 2003.

[21] Brühlmeier, 2010.

[22] Lane, 1975.

[23] Montessori, 2003, p. 13.

[24] Montessori, 1967.

[25] Ashton-Warner, 1966.

[26] Boser, Wilhelm, & Hanna, 2014.

[27] American Psychological Association Zero Tolerance Task Force, 2008.

[28] Addams, 1909.

[29] Shareski, 2017; Walker, 2017.

[30] Hall, 1904.

[31] James, 1984.

[32] Damon, 2008.

[33] Zedelius, Müller, & Schooler, 2017.

[34] Brendtro, 1988.

[35] Berry & Frederickson, 2015.

[36] Chambers & Freado, 2015.

[37] Laursen, 2018, p. 122.

[38] Long, Wood, & Fecser, 2001.

[39] Peterson, 2013.

[40] American Psychiatric Association, 2013.

[41] Edens & Cahill, 2007.

[42] Frances, 2013.

[43] Foltz, Dang, Daniels, Doyle, McFee, & Quisenberry, 2013.

[44] Maslow, 1970.

[45] Wilker, 1993.

[46] Hallahan, Kauffman, & Pullen, 2013, p. 160.

[47] As cited in Key, 1909.

[48] Dewey, 1916.

[49] Benedict, 1938.

[50] Rousseau, 1979, p. 89.

[51] Du Bois, 1909, p. 235.

[52] Rousseau, 1979.

[53] Coopersmith, 1967.

[54] Seita, 2014.

[55] Olweus, 1993.

[56] Juvonen & Graham, 2013.

[57] Baumrind, 2013.

[58] Larson & Brendtro, 2000.

[59] Seita, 2012, p. 35.

[60] Frankl, 2006.

[61] Damon, 2008, p. 179.

[62] As cited in Ayers, 2003, p. 428.

[63] National Archives, n.d.

[64] Block, 2009.

[65] Putnam, 2000.

[66] Block, 2009, p. 1.

[67] Block, 2009, p. 51.

[68] Turkle, 2017.

[69] Colvin, 2015.

[70] Wilkinson & Pickett, 2011.

[71] As cited in Treasurer, 2003, p. 222.

[72] Kielsmeier, Scales, Roehlkepartain, & Neal, 2004.

[73] Benson, Williams, & Johnson, 1987.

[74] Ryan & Deci, 2017, p. 226.

[75] Charleston, 1989.

[76] Bryk & Schneider, 2002.

[77] Payne, 1875, p. 84.

[78] Owens & Valesky, 2014.

[79] Guthrie & Schuermann, 2011, p. 8.

[80] Van Bockern, 2018.

Chapter 4

[1] As cited in Tragaskis, 2015.

[2] Baumeister, 2012.

[3] Ryan & Deci, 2017, p. 10.

[4] McDonald, 2013.

[5] Bryk et al., 2010.

[6] Cassidy & Shaver, 2018, p. xi.

[7] Ainsworth & Bowlby, 1991.

[8] Ainsworth, Blehar, Waters, & Wall, 1978.

[9] K. Juul, personal communication, 1985.

[10] Gibbs, 2014.

[11] Korczak, 1967.

[12] Hernandez, 2016, p. 1.

[13] Hernandez, 2016, p. 5.

[14] Hernandez, 2016, p. 121.

[15] Brown & Seita, 2010.

[16] Cournos, 2000

[17] Cournos, 2000, p. 100.

[18] Seita & Brendtro, 2005.

[19] Gottman, 2011.

[20] Digney, 2013.

[21] Gottman, 2011.

[22] Parker, 2019.

[23] Cassidy & Shaver, 2018.

[24] Milliken, 2007, p. 3.

[25] Jensen, 2019.

[26] Hobbs, 1994, p. 22.

[27] Seita & Brendtro, 2005.

[28] J. Odney, personal communication, June 1992.

[29] Porges, 2018.

[30] Janak & Tye, 2015.

[31] Garfat, Freeman, Gharabaghi, & Fulcher, 2018.

[32] Duncan, Miller, Wampold, & Hubble, 2010.

[33] Hall, 1829, p. 47.

[34] Redl & Wineman, 1952.

[35] Cozolino, 2014, p. 34.

[36] Perry & Szalavitz, 2017, p. 230.

[37] Sue, 2010.

[38] Hardy, 2013.

[39] Odney & Brendtro, 1992, p. 5.

Chapter 5

[1] Golinkoff & Hirsh-Pasek, 2016, p. 247.

[2] de Montaigne, 1877.

[3] Cajete, 1994.

[4] Rogoff, Mejía-Arauz, & Correa-Chávez, 2015.

[5] Coyle, 2009.

[6] Golinkoff & Hirsh-Pasek, 2016, p. 219.

[7] As cited in Gorman, 2018.

[8] Hemingway, 1929, p. 318.

[9] Brendtro & Mitchell, 2015.

[10] Perry & Hambrick, 2008, p. 39.

[11] Costandi, 2016.

[12] Siegel, 2012.

[13] Doidge, 2015.

[14] Neufeld & Maté, 2005.

[15] Krisberg, 2005.

[16] American Psychological Association, 2012.

[17] Siegel, 2015.

[18] Ewert & Sibthorp, 2014.

[19] Francis, 2011.

[20] Hall, 2012.

[21] ENCODE Project, 2018.

[22] Francis, 2011.

[23] Carey, 2012.

[24] Grandjean & Landrigan, 2014.

[25] Csoka & Szyf, 2009, p. 771.

[26] Allen Institute of Brain Sciences, 2012.

[27] Rutter, 2012.

[28] McEwen, 2008.

[29] Felitti & Anda, 2010.

[30] Meaney, 2001.

[31] Costandi, 2016.

[32] Pember, 2017.

[33] Brave Heart, 2003.

[34] Pleuss & Belsky, 2015.

[35] Sugden, Arseneault, Harrington, Moffitt, Williams, & Caspi, 2010.

[36] Pleuss & Belsky, 2015.

[37] Nelson, Fox, & Zeanah, 2014.

[38] Steinberg, 2014.

[39] As cited in Shapiro, 2006, p. 705.

[40] Purvis, Cross, & Lyons-Sunshine, 2007.

[41] van der Kolk, 2014.

[42] Explo, n.d.

[43] Goleman, 2006.

[44] Lantieri, 2001, p. 33.

[45] Costandi, 2016.

[46] Walker, 2017.

[47] Siegel, 2010.

[48] Watanabe-Crockett, 2019.

[49] Lantieri, 2014.

[50] Cozolino, 2014, p. 203.

[51] Perry, 2001.

[52] Brendtro, 2016.

[53] Bath & Seita, 2018.

[54] Bath & Seita, 2018, p. 101.

[55] Dewey, 1916.

[56] McNulty & Quaglia, 2007).

[57] Kolb & Kolb, 2017.

[58] As cited in Zimmers, 1918, p. 17.

[59] Dewey, 1990, p. 29.

[60] Stack Exchange, n.d.

[61] Zeigarnik, 1927.

[62] Nichols & Berliner, 2007.

[63] Duckenfield & Drew, 2006.

[64] Roediger, McDermott, & McDaniel, 2011.

[65] Bjork & Bjork, 2015.

[66] Reyna, Chapman, Dougherty, & Confrey, 2012.

[67] Van Bockern, 2018, p. 33.

[68] Nicholls, 1992.

[69] Csikszentmihalyi, 2007.

[70] Duckworth, 2016.

[71] Dweck, 2016.

[72] Dweck, 2016, p. 229.

[73] Dweck, 2016, p. 229.

[74] Costandi, 2016, p. 86.

[75] Zynga, 2014.

[76] Novak & Slattery, 2017; Stobaugh, 2019.

[77] Smith, 2009, p. 123.

[78] Durlak, Weissberg, Dymnicki, Taylor, & Schellinger, 2011.

[79] Gambone, Klem, & Connell, 2002.

[80] Slavin, 2005.

[81] Slavin, 1995.

[82] Slavin, Hurley, &
    Chamberlain, 2003.

[83] Griffin, 2008; Johnson,
    Johnson, & Stanne, 1986.

[84] Aronson & Patnoe, 2011.

[85] Jigsaw Classroom, n.d.

[86] Condensed from Aronson &
    Patnoe, 2011, pp. 111–112.

Chapter 6

[1] Montessori, 1949, p. 27.

[2] Benedict, 1938.

[3] Korczak, 1986.

[4] Brendtro & Larson, 2006.

[5] Pink, 2009.

[6] Durkin, 1988, p. 361.

[7] Murphy & Moriarity, 1976.

[8] As cited in Johnson, 2006, p. 88.

[9] Bath & Seita, 2018.

[10] Bath & Seita, 2018.

[11] Bandura, 1997.

[12] Seligman, 2011.

[13] Keltner, 2016.

[14] Stott, 1982, p. 305.

[15] Coopersmith, 1967.

[16] Wills, 1941.

[17] As cited in Dreikurs, 1971.

[18] Tate, Copas, & Wasmund, 2012.

[19] Makarenko, 1951.

[20] Greenleaf, 2002.

[21] Lewin, 1999.

[22] Hoffman, 2000.

[23] Garfat, Fulcher, & Digney, 2013.

[24] Bernard & Kurlychek, 2010.

[25] Adorno, Frenkel-Brunswik,
    Levinson, & Sanford, 1950.

[26] Frances, 2017; Fromm, 1941.

[27] Don Bosco West, 2000.

[28] Hibbing, Smith, & Alford, 2014.

[29] Feldman & Stenner, 1997.

[30] Gold & Osgood, 1992.

[31] Baumrind, 2013.

[32] Baumrind, 2008.

[33] Chen, Dong, & Zhou, 1997.

[34] Ryan & Deci, 2017.

[35] Hafen, Allen, Mikami, Gregory,
    Hamre, & Pianta, 2012.

[36] Gold & Osgood, 1992.

[37] Quigley, 2014.

[38] As cited in Whelan, 1998.

[39] Laursen & Tate, 2012.

[40] Brendtro, 2004.

[41] Rousseau, 1979, p. 101.

[42] Gibbs, 2014.

[43] Dreikurs, Grunwald, &
    Pepper, 1982.

[44] Davis, 2014.

[45] Bergin, 2018.

[46] Brendtro & Bath, 2019.

[47] Long, 2014.

[48] Long, 2015, p. 13.

[49] Bradley, 2003.

[50] Taylor, 2002.

[51] Brendtro & du Toit, 2005.

[52] Taylor, 2002.

[53] Dewey, 1910, pp. 113, 130.

[54] Bath & Seita, 2018.

[55] Panksepp & Biven, 2012.

[56] Koehler & Seger, 2011.

[57] Morse, 2008.

Chapter 7

[1] Damon, 2008, p. 40.

[2] Gray, 2013.

[3] Spencer, 1864, p. 444.

[4] Keltner, 2009.

[5] Darwin, 1871, p. 130.

[6] Hall, 1904.

[7] Addams, 1909, p. 161.

[8] As cited in Holman, 1908,
    pp. 250–251.

[9] Batson, 2011.

[10] Wallach & Wallach, 1983.

[11] Gibbs, 2014.

[12] Fuster, 2015.

[13] Gibbs, 2003.

[14] Bronfenbrenner, 2005.

[15] Bronfenbrenner, 2005, p. 254.

[16] Hahn, 1959, p. 6.

[17] Roehlkepartain, King, Wagener, & Benson, 2006.

[18] Kielsmeier et al., 2004.

[19] Selye, 1974.

[20] Churchill, 2011.

[21] Brendtro & Bath, 2019.

[22] Kaye, 2010.

[23] Slavson, 1965, p. 22.

[24] Brendtro, 2019.

[25] Prouty, Panicucci, & Collinson, 2007.

[26] As cited in Prouty et al., 2007, p. 3.

[27] Gharabaghi, 2014.

[28] Bear, Whitcomb, Elias, & Blank, 2015.

[29] American Psychological Association Zero Tolerance Task Force, 2008.

[30] U.S. Department of Education, 2010.

[31] Sugai & Horner, 2009.

[32] SEL is promoted by CASEL, the Collaborative for Academic, Social, and Emotional Learning (https://casel.org).

[33] Bear et al., 2015

[34] Durlak, Weissberg, Dymnicki, Taylor, & Schellinger, 2011.

[35] Bear et al., 2015.

[36] Li & Julian, 2012.

[37] Osher & Berg, 2018.

[38] Bergin, 2018.

[39] Kohn, 2015.

[40] Kohn, 2018.

[41] Cozolino, 2014, p. 4.

[42] Noddings, 2013.

[43] Van Bockern, 2018.

[44] Buffum, Mattos, & Malone, 2018.

[45] Buffum et al., 2018, p. 18.

[46] Brendtro & Freado, 2018.

[47] Li & Julian, 2012.

[48] Dodge, Dishion, & Lansford, 2006.

[49] Longhurst & McCord, 2014.

[50] Henggeler, Schoenwald, Borduin, Rowland, & Cunningham, 1998, p. 151.

[51] Brendtro & Mitchell, 2015; Gibbs, Potter, & Goldstein, 1995; Gold & Osgood, 1992; James, 2011; Vorrath & Brendtro, 1985.

[52] California Evidence-Based Clearinghouse, 2018.

[53] Allen, 2015.

[54] Tate et al., 2012.

[55] Brendtro & Bath, 2019.

[56] Project Förderende, 2017.

[57] Longhurst & McCord, 2014.

[58] Laursen, 2010.

[59] Project Förderende, 2017.

[60] Montessori, 2003.

[61] As cited in Messerli, 1972.

[62] Key, 1909, p. 185.

[63] Brendtro & Hinders, 1990.

[64] As cited in Korzcak, 1967, p. v.

[65] Key, 1909.

Chapter 8

[1] van der Kolk, 2014, p. 278.

[2] Werner & Smith, 1977, 1982, 1992, 2001.

[3] Condensed from Werner, 2012.

[4] Garmezy & Rutter, 1983.

[5] Rutter, O'Connor, & English and Romanian Adoptees (ERA) Study Team, 2004.

[6] White, 1959.

[7] Bandura, 1997; van der Kolk, 2007.

[8] Cicchetti & Valentino, 2006, p. 165.

[9] Ross, 2009.

[10] Kirmayer, Gone, & Moses, 2014.

[11] Davenport, 1648.

[12] Dunbar-Ortiz, 2014.

[13] Woods, 2017, p. 68.

[14] Freire, 2018.

[15] Johansen, 2012.

[16] Gone, 2015.

References and Resources

Addams, J. (1909). *The spirit of youth and the city streets.* New York: Macmillan.

Adler, A. (1930). *The problem child.* New York: Putnam's Sons.

Adler, M. J. (1985). *Ten philosophical mistakes.* New York: Macmillan.

Adorno, T. W., Frenkel-Brunswik, E., Levinson, D. J., & Sanford, R. N. (1950). *The authoritarian personality.* New York: Harper.

Ainsworth, M., Blehar, M. C., Waters, E., & Wall, S. (1978). *Patterns of attachment: A psychological study of the strange situation.* Hillsdale, NJ: Erlbaum.

Ainsworth, M., & Bowlby, J. (1991). An ethological approach to personality development. *American Psychologist, 46*(4), 333–346.

Allen, D. (2015). Empowering youth to make responsible decisions. *Reclaiming Children and Youth, 23*(4), 36–38.

Allen Institute of Brain Science. (2012, September 19). Human brains share a consistent genetic blueprint and possess enormous biochemical complexity. *Science Daily.* Accessed at www.sciencedaily.com/releases /2012/09/120919135318.htm on January 4, 2019.

American Psychiatric Association. (2013). *Diagnostic and statistical manual of mental disorders* (5th ed.). Washington, DC: Author.

American Psychological Association. (2012). Supreme Court of the United States. Brief for the American Psychological Association, American Psychiatric Association, and National Association of Social Workers as amici curiae in support of petitioners Evan Miller and Kuntrell Jackson. In *Evan Miller v. Alabama and Kuntrell Jackson v. Ray Hobbs, 567 U.S. 460* (2012).

American Psychological Association Presidential Task Force on Evidence-Based Practice. (2006). Evidence-based practice in psychology. *American Psychologist, 61*(4), 271–285.

American Psychological Association Zero Tolerance Task Force. (2008). Are zero tolerance policies effective in schools? *American Psychologist, 63*(9), 852–862.

Anglin, J. P. (2002). *Pain, normality, and the struggle for congruence: Reinterpreting residential care for children and youth.* Binghamton, NY: Haworth Press.

Anglin, J. P., & Brendtro, L. K. (2017). Enduring wisdom: Towards a comprehensive history of professional child and youth care. *Scottish Journal of Residential Child Care, 16*(3). Accessed at www.celcis.org/files /7615/1265/4669/2017_Vol_16_3_Anglin_J_Enduring_wisdom.pdf on January 4, 2019.

Aronson, E., & Patnoe, S. (2011). *Cooperation in the classroom: The jigsaw method* (3rd ed.). New York: Pinter & Martin.

Ashton-Warner, S. (1966). *Teacher.* New York: Simon & Schuster.

Ayers, W. B. (2003). *The United States government: A citizen's inquiry into what it is and might be.* Raleigh, NC: Ivy House.

Bandura, A. (1997). *Self-efficacy: The exercise of control.* New York: Worth.

Bath, H., & Seita, J. R. (2018). *The three pillars of transforming care: Trauma and resilience in the other 23 hours.* Winnipeg, Canada: University of Winnipeg Faculty of Education.

Batson, C. D. (2011). *Altruism in humans.* New York: Oxford University Press.

Baumeister, R. F. (2012). Need-to-belong theory. In P. A. M. Van Lange, A. W. Kruglanski, & E. T. Higgins (Eds.), *The handbook of theories of social psychology* (Vol. 2, pp. 121–140). Thousand Oaks, CA: SAGE.

Baumrind, D. (2008). Authoritative parenting for character and competence. In D. Streight (Ed.), *Parenting for character: Five experts, five practices* (pp. 15–30). Portland, OR: Council for Spiritual and Ethical Education.

Baumrind, D. (2013). Authoritative parenting revisited: History and current status. In R. E. Larzelere, A. S. Morris, & A. W. Harrist (Eds.), *Authoritative parenting: Synthesizing nurturance and discipline for optimal child development* (pp. 11–34). Washington, DC: American Psychological Association.

Bear, G. G., Whitcomb, S. A., Elias, M. J., & Blank, J. C. (2015). SEL and schoolwide positive behavioral interventions and supports. In J. A. Durlak, C. E. Domitrovich, R. P. Weissberg, & T. P. Gullotta (Eds.), *Handbook of social and emotional learning* (pp. 453–467). New York: Guilford Press.

Benard, B. (2004). *Resiliency: What we have learned.* San Francisco: WestEd.

Benedict, R. (1938). Continuities and discontinuities in cultural conditioning. *Psychiatry: Interpersonal and Biological Processes, 1*(2), 161–167.

Benson, P., Williams, D., & Johnson, A. (1987). *The quicksilver years: The hopes and fears of early adolescence.* San Francisco: Harper & Row.

Bergin, C. (2018). *Designing a prosocial classroom: Growing kinder students from pre-K–12 with the curriculum you already use*. New York: Norton.

Bernard, T., & Kurlychek, M. (2010). *The cycle of juvenile justice*. New York: Oxford University Press.

Berry, Z., & Frederickson, J. (2015). Explanations and implications of the fundamental attribution error. *Journal of Integrated Social Sciences*, *5*(1), 44–57. Accessed at www.jiss.org/documents/volume_5/issue_1 on January 7, 2019.

Bertolino, R. (2014). *Thriving on the front lines: A guide to strengths-based youth care work*. New York: Routledge.

Bird-David, N. (2017). Studying children in "hunter-gatherer" societies. In B. S. Hewlett & M. E. Lamb (Eds.), *Hunter-gatherer childhoods: Evolutionary, developmental and cultural perspectives* (pp. 92–101). New York: Routledge.

Bjork, E. L., & Bjork, R. A. (2015). Making things hard on yourself, but in a good way: Creating desirable difficulties to enhance learning. In M. A. Gernsbacher & J. R. Pomerantz (Eds.), *Psychology and the real world: Essays illustrating fundamental contributions to society* (2nd ed., pp. 60–68). New York: Worth.

Black Elk. (1932). *Black Elk speaks*. New York: Morrow.

Block, P. (2009). *Community: The structure of belonging*. San Francisco: Berrett-Koehler.

Blue Bird, G. (2012). Decolonization lessons for tribal prisoners. In Waziyatawin & M. Yellow Bird (Eds.), *For Indigenous minds only: A decolonization handbook* (pp. 205–224). Santa Fe, NM: School for Advanced Research Press.

Blumenkrantz, D. G. (2016). *Coming of age the RITE way: Youth and community development through rites of passage*. New York: Oxford University Press.

Boehm, C. (2012). *Moral origins: The evolution of virtue, altruism, and shame*. New York: Basic Books.

Bolin, I. (2006). *Growing up in a culture of respect: Child rearing in highland Peru*. Austin, TX: University of Texas Press.

Bolin, I. (2010). Chillihuani's culture of respect and the Circle of Courage. *Reclaiming Children and Youth*, *18*(4), 12–17.

Boser, U., Wilhelm, M., & Hanna, R. (2014, October 6). *The power of the Pygmalion effect.* Washington, DC: Center for American Progress. Accessed at www.americanprogress.org/issues/education-k-12/reports/2014/10/06 /96806/the-power-of-the-pygmalion-effect on January 7, 2019.

Bowlby, J. (1988). *A secure base: Parent-child attachment and healthy human development.* New York: Basic Books.

Bradley, S. J. (2003). *Affect regulation and the development of psychopathology.* New York: Guilford Press.

Brave Heart, M. Y. (2003). The historical trauma response among Natives and its relationship with substance abuse: A Lakota illustration. *Journal of Psychoactive Drugs, 35*(1), 7–13.

Brendtro, L. K. (1988). Problems as opportunity: Developing positive theories about troubled youth. *Journal of Child Care, 3*(6), 15–24.

Brendtro, L. K. (2004, January 15). *From coercive to strength-based intervention: Responding to the needs of children in pain.* Presented with Charles Curie at Children and Youth: Their Needs, Our Commitment, a conference of the Alliance for Children and Families, Naples Beach, Florida. Accessed at http://nospank.net/brendtro.pdf on January 7, 2019.

Brendtro, L. K. (2016). Touch: The foundation of belonging. *Thriving, 1*(8), 1–9. Accessed at http://growingedgetraining.com/wp-content/uploads /2017/10/Touch-Foundation-of-Belonging_Thriving_vol_1-8.pdf on May 1, 2019.

Brendtro, L. K. (2019). Generosity: Building circles of respect. *Thriving, 4*(3), 1–9.

Brendtro, L. K., & Bath, H. (2019). *Respectful alliances: Positive peer cultures and inspired staff teams.* Lennox, SD: Resilience Resources.

Brendtro, L. K., & du Toit, L. (2005). *Response ability pathways (RAP): Restoring bonds of respect.* Cape Town, South Africa: Pretext.

Brendtro, L. K., & Freado, M. (2018). *Planning restorative outcomes: Assessment of strengths and needs* [Certification training]. Lennox, SD: Reclaiming Youth at Risk. Accessed at https://reclaimingyouthatrisk.org/courses/planning -restorative-outcomes on January 7, 2019.

Brendtro, L. K., & Hinders, D. (1990). Essay reviews: A saga of Janusz Korczak, the king of children. *Harvard Educational Review, 60*(2), 237–246.

Brendtro, L. K., & Larson, S. J. (2006). *The resilience revolution: Discovering strengths in challenging kids.* Bloomington, IN: Solution Tree Press.

Brendtro, L. K., & Mitchell, M. L. (2015). *Deep brain learning: Evidence-based essentials in education, treatment, and youth development*. Albion, MI: Starr Commonwealth.

Brendtro, L. K., & Ness, A. E. (1983). *Re-educating troubled youth: Environments for teaching and treatment*. New York: Routledge.

Brokenleg, M. (2010). The resilience revolution: Our original collaboration. *Reclaiming Children and Youth, 18*(4), 8–11.

Brokenleg, M. (2014). Restoring bonds of respect. *Reclaiming Children and Youth, 22*(4), 12–13.

Brokenleg, M., & James, A. B. (2013). Living in balance: A Lakota and Mohawk dialogue. *Reclaiming Children and Youth, 22*(2), 51–55.

Bronfenbrenner, U. (1979). *The ecology of human development: Experiments by nature and design*. Cambridge, MA: Harvard University Press.

Bronfenbrenner, U. (1986). Alienation and the four worlds of childhood. *Phi Delta Kappan, 67*(6), 430–436.

Bronfenbrenner, U. (Ed.). (2005). *Making human beings human: Bioecological perspectives on human development*. Thousand Oaks, CA: SAGE.

Brown, W. K., & Seita, J. R. (2010). *Growing up in the care of strangers: The experiences, insights and recommendations of eleven former foster kids*. Tallahassee, FL: Gladden Foundation Press.

Brühlmeier, A. (2010). *Head, heart and hand: Education in the spirit of Pestalozzi*. Cambridge, England: Sophia Books.

Bryde, J. F. (1971). *Indian students and guidance*. Boston: Houghton Mifflin.

Bryk, A. S., & Schneider, B. (2002). *Trust in schools: A core resource for improvement*. New York: Sage Foundation.

Bryk, A. S., Sebring, P. B., Allensworth, E., Luppescu, S., & Easton, J. Q. (2010). *Organizing schools for improvement: Lessons from Chicago*. Chicago: University of Chicago Press.

Buffum, A., Mattos, M., & Malone, J. (2018). *Taking action: A handbook for RTI at Work*. Bloomington, IN: Solution Tree Press.

Cajete, G. A. (1994). *Look to the mountain: An ecology of Indigenous education*. Durango, CO: Kivaki Press.

Cajete, G. A. (2000). *Native science: Natural laws of interdependence*. Santa Fe, NM: Clear Light.

Cajete, G. A. (2012). Decolonizing Indigenous education in a twenty-first century world. In Waziyatawin & M. Yellow Bird (Eds.), *For Indigenous eyes only: A decolonization handbook* (pp. 145–156). Santa Fe, NM: School for Advanced Research Press.

Cajete, G. A. (2015). *Indigenous community: Rekindling the teachings of the Seventh Fire*. St. Paul, MN: Living Justice Press.

California Evidence-Based Clearinghouse. (2018). *Positive peer culture*. Accessed at www.cebc4cw.org/program/positive-peer-culture on January 7, 2019.

Callahan, K. L. (2010). *The path of the medicine wheel: A guide to the sacred circle*. Victoria, Canada: Trafford.

Carey, N. (2012). *The epigenetics revolution: How modern biology is rewriting our understanding of genetics, disease, and inheritance*. New York: Columbia University Press.

Cassidy, J., & Shaver, P. R. (Eds.). (2018). *Handbook of attachment: Theory, research, and clinical applications* (3rd ed.). New York: Guilford Press.

Caycedo, G. C. (1977). *Colombia amarga*. Bogotá, Colombia: Valencia Editores.

Chambers, J., & Freado, M. (2015). *The art of kid whispering: Reaching the inside kid*. Sioux Falls, SD: Authors.

Charleston, S. (1989). The tyranny of time. *Lutheran Woman Today, 2*(7), 27–32.

Chen, X., Dong, Q., & Zhou, H. (1997). Authoritative and authoritarian parenting practices and social and school performance in Chinese children. *International Journal of Behavioral Development, 21*(4), 855–873.

Cheng, W., Rolls, E. T., Huaguang, G., Zhang, J., & Feng, J. (2015). Autism: Reduced connectivity between cortical areas involved in face expression, theory of mind, and the sense of self. *Brain, 138*(5), 1382–1393.

Churchill, P. (2011). *Braintrust: What neuroscience tells us about morality*. Princeton, NJ: Princeton University Press.

Cicchetti, D., & Valentino, K. (2006). An ecological-transactional perspective on child maltreatment: Failure of the average expectable environment and its influence on child development. In D. Cicchetti & D. J. Cohen (Eds.), *Developmental psychopathology: Risk, disorder, and adaptation* (2nd ed., Vol. 3, pp. 129–201). Hoboken, NJ: Wiley.

Collier, J. (1947). *The Indians of the Americas*. New York: Norton.

Colvin, G. (2015). *Humans are underrated: What high achievers know that brilliant machines never will*. New York: Portfolio.

Common Ground. (n.d.) *The stolen generations*. Accessed at www.commonground
.org.au/learn/the-stolen-generations on February 19, 2019.

Coolidge, F. L., & Wynn, T. (2018). *The rise of homo sapiens: The evolution of
modern thinking*. New York: Oxford University Press.

Coopersmith, S. (1967). *The antecedents of self-esteem*. San Francisco: Freeman.

Costandi, M. (2016). *Neuroplasticity*. Cambridge, MA: Massachusetts Institute
for Technology Press.

Cournos, F. (2000). *City of one: A memoir*. New York: Norton.

Coyle, D. (2009). *The talent code: Greatness isn't born. It's grown. Here's how*.
New York: Bantam Books.

Cozolino, L. (2014). *Attachment-based teaching: Creating a tribal classroom*.
New York: Norton.

Cross, T. L. (2012). *Relational worldview model*. Portland, OR: National Indian
Child Welfare Association. Accessed at www.sprc.org/sites/default/files
/resource-program/Relational-Worldview-Model.pdf on January 7, 2019.

Csikszentmihalyi, M. (2007). *Flow: The psychology of optimal experience*. New
York: Harper Perennial.

Csoka, A. B., & Szyf, M. (2009). Epigenetic side-effects of common
pharmaceuticals: A potential new field in medicine and pharmacology.
Medical Hypotheses, 73(5), 770–780.

Damon, W. (2008). *The path to purpose: Helping our children find their calling
in life*. New York: Free Press.

Darwin, C. (1871). *The descent of man*. Princeton, NJ: Princeton University Press.

Davenport, F. G. (Ed.). (1648). *European treaties bearing on the history of the United
States and its dependencies to 1648*. Washington, DC: Carnegie Institution
of Washington, 1917, 61–63. Accessed at www.encyclopediavirginia.org
/Inter_caetera_by_Pope_Alexander_VI_May_4_1493 on February 27, 2019.

Davis, F. (2014). Discipline with dignity: Oakland classrooms try healing
instead of punishment. *Reclaiming Children and Youth, 23*(1), 38–41.

Deloria, E. (1998). *Speaking of Indians*. Lincoln, NE: Bison Books.

Deloria, V., Jr. (2009). *C. J. Jung and the Sioux traditions: Dreams, visions, nature,
and the primitive*. P. Deloria & J. Bernstein (Eds.). New Orleans, LA: Spring
Journal Books.

Deloria, V., Jr., & Wildcat, D. R. (2001). *Power and place: Indian education in
America*. Golden, CO: Fulcrum Resources.

de Montaigne, M. (1877). On the education of children. In *Essays of Michel de Montaigne* (C. Cotton, Trans.). Accessed at www.gutenberg.org/files /3600/3600-h/3600-h.htm on January 7, 2019.

Densmore, F. (1929). Chippewa customs. *Bureau of American Ethnology Bulletin, 86.* Washington, DC: Smithsonian Institution.

Dewey, J. (1910). *How we think.* Boston: Heath.

Dewey, J. (1916). *Democracy and education.* New York: Macmillan.

Dewey, J. (1990). *The school and society and the child and the curriculum.* Chicago: University of Chicago Press.

Digney, J. (2013). Making humor meaningful in child and youth care: A personal reflection. In T. Garfat, L. Fulcher, & J. Digney (Eds.), *Making moments meaningful in child and youth care practice* (pp. 119–124). Cape Town, South Africa: Pretext.

Dodge, K. A., Dishion, T. J., & Lansford, J. E. (Eds.). (2006). *Deviant peer influence in programs for youth: Problems and solutions* (pp. 141–161). New York: Guilford Press.

Doidge, N. (2015). *The brain's way of healing: Remarkable discoveries and recoveries from the frontiers of neuroplasticity.* New York: Penguin.

Don Bosco West. (2000). *The Salesian preventive system of St. John Bosco: Don Bosco's way, style, approach, method, system, etc. of educating and accompanying young people today.* Accessed at www.donboscowest.org/pedagogy /preventive-system on January 7, 2019.

Dreikurs, R. (1971). *Social equality: The challenge of today.* Chicago: Regnery.

Dreikurs, R., Grunwald, B. B., & Pepper, F. C. (1982). *Maintaining sanity in the classroom: Classroom management techniques* (2nd ed.). New York: Harper & Row.

Du Bois, W. E. B. (1909). *John Brown.* Philadelphia: Jacobs.

Duckenfield, M., & Drew, S. (2006). Measure what matters and no child will be left behind. In J. C. Kielsmeier, M. Neal, & A. Crossley (Eds.), *Growing to greatness: The state of service-learning project* (pp. 33–39). St. Paul, MN: National Youth Leadership Council.

Duckworth, A. (2016). *Grit: The power of passion and perseverance.* New York: Scribner.

Dunbar-Ortiz, R. (2014). *An Indigenous peoples' history of the United States.* Boston: Beacon Press.

Duncan, B. L., Miller, S. D., Wampold, B. E., & Hubble, M. A. (Eds.). (2010), *The heart and soul of change: Delivering what works in therapy* (2nd ed.). Washington, DC: American Psychological Association.

Durkin, R. (1988). Restructuring for competence: A case for the democratization and communitization of children's programs. In R. Small & F. Alwon (Eds.), *Challenging the limits of care* (pp. 353–367). Needham, MA: Trieschman Center.

Durlak, J. A., Weissberg, R. P., Dymnicki, A. B., Taylor, R. D., & Schellinger, K. B. (2011). The impact of enhancing students' social and emotional learning: A meta-analysis of school-based universal interventions. *Child Development, 82*(1), 405–432.

Dweck, C. S. (2016). *Mindset: The new psychology of success* (Updated ed.). New York: Random House.

Eastman, C. A. (1902). *Indian boyhood.* New York: McClure, Philips.

Eastman, C. A. (1911). *The soul of the Indian: An interpretation.* New York: Houghton Mifflin.

Eastman, C. A. (1919). Opening address, Society of American Indians, October 2, Minneapolis, MN. *The American Indian Magazine, 3,* 145–152.

Eastman, C. A. (2010). *Living in two worlds: The American Indian experience* (M. O. Fitzgerald, Ed.). Bloomington, IN: World Wisdom Press.

Edens, J. F., & Cahill, M. A. (2007). Psychopathy in adolescence and criminal recidivism in young adulthood: Longitudinal results from a multiethnic sample of youthful offenders. *Assessment, 14*(1), 57–64.

Einstein, A. (1954). *Ideas and opinions.* New York: Three Rivers Press.

Elias, M. J., Leverett, L., Duffell, J. C., Humphrey, N., Stepney, C., & Ferrito, J. (2015). Integrating SEL with related prevention and youth development approaches. In J. A. Durlak, C. E. Domitrovich, R. P. Weissberg, & T. P. Gullotta (Eds.), *Handbook of social and emotional learning* (pp. 33–49). New York: Guilford Press.

Elliot, A. J. (2006). The hierarchical model of approach-avoidance motivation. *Motivation and Emotion, 30*(2), 111–116.

ENCODE Project. (2018). *The ENCODE project: ENCyclopedia of DNA elements.* Accessed at www.genome.gov/10005107/the-encode-project -encyclopedia-of-dna-elements on January 7, 2019.

Erikson, E. H. (1963). *Childhood and society* (2nd ed.). New York: Norton.

Espiner, D., & Guild, D. (2018). *Rolling with resilience: Building family strengths*. Auckland, New Zealand: Connections That Count Trust NZ.

Ewert, A. W., & Sibthorp, J. (2014). *Outdoor education: Foundations, theory, and research*. Champaign, IL: Human Kinetics.

Explo. (n.d.) *Abraham Maslow quote* [Blog post]. Accessed at https://blog.explo.org/abraham-maslow-quote on April 16, 2019.

Feldman, S., & Stenner, K. (1997). Perceived threat and authoritarianism. *Political Psychology, 18*(4), 741–770.

Felitti, V. J., & Anda, R. F. (2010). The relationship of adverse childhood experiences to adult medical disease, psychiatric disorder and sexual behavior: Implications for healthcare. In R. A. Lanius, E. Vermetten, & C. Pain (Eds.), *The impact of early life trauma on health and disease: The hidden epidemic* (pp. 77–87). Cambridge, England: Cambridge University Press.

Fisher, D., & Frey, N. (2014). *Better learning through structured teaching: A framework for the gradual release of responsibility* (2nd ed.). Alexandria, VA: Association for Supervision and Curriculum Development.

Foltz, R., Brendtro, L. K., & Mitchell, M. L. (2015). The vital balance. In L. K. Brendtro & M. L. Mitchell (Eds.), *Deep brain learning: Evidence-based essentials in education, treatment, and youth development* (pp. 96–112). Albion, MI: Starr Commonwealth.

Foltz, R., Dang, S., Daniels, B., Doyle, H., McFee, S., & Quisenberry, C. (2013). When diagnostic labels mask trauma. *Reclaiming Children and Youth, 22*(2), 12–17.

Frances, A. (2013). *Saving normal: An insider's revolt against out-of-control psychiatric diagnosis, DSM-5, big pharma, and the medicalization of ordinary life*. New York: Morrow.

Frances, A. (2017). *Twilight of American sanity*. New York: HarperCollins.

Francis, R. C. (2011). *Epigenetics: How environment shapes our genes*. New York: Norton.

Frankl, V. E. (2006). *Man's search for meaning*. Boston: Beacon Press.

Freado, M. D. (2017). Hitting the right chord: The six keys to thriving. *Thriving, 2*(15). Accessed at http://growingedgetraining.com/wp-content/uploads/2017/10/Hitting-the-Right-Chord_vol_2-15.pdf on January 7, 2019.

Freire, P. (2018). *Pedagogy of the oppressed* (50th anniversary ed.). New York: Bloomsbury Academic.

Fromm, E. (1941). *Escape from freedom*. New York: Farrar & Rinehart.

Fuster, J. M. (2015). *The prefrontal cortex* (5th ed.). Cambridge, MA: Academic Press.

Gambone, M. A., Klem, A. M., & Connell, J. P. (2002). *Finding out what matters for youth: Testing key links in a community action framework for youth development*. Philadelphia: Youth Development Strategies.

Garfat, T., Freeman, J., Gharabaghi, K., & Fulcher, L. (2018). Characteristics of a relational child and youth care approach. *CYC-Online, 236*, 7–46.

Garfat, T., Fulcher, L., & Digney, J. (Eds.). (2013). *Making moments meaningful in child and youth care practice*. Cape Town, South Africa: CYC-Net Press.

Garmezy, N., & Rutter, M. (Eds.). (1983). *Stress, coping, and development in children*. New York: McGraw-Hill.

Gharabaghi, K. (2014). The purpose of youth work. In K. Gharabaghi, H. A. Skott-Myhre, & M. Krueger (Eds.), *With children and youth: Emerging theories and practices in child and youth care work* (pp. 3–24). Waterloo, Canada: Laurier University Press.

Gibbs, J. C. (2003). Equipping youth with mature moral judgment. *Reclaiming Children and Youth, 12*(3), 148–153

Gibbs, J. C. (2014). *Moral development and reality: Beyond the theories of Kohlberg, Hoffman, and Haidt* (3rd ed.). New York: Oxford University Press.

Gibbs, J. C., Potter, G. B., & Goldstein, A. P. (1995). *The EQUIP program: Teaching youth to think and act responsibly through a peer-helping approach*. Champaign, IL: Research Press.

Gluckman, P., & Hanson, M. (2006). *Mismatch: Why our world no longer fits our bodies*. Oxford, England: Oxford University Press.

Gold, M., & Osgood, D. W. (1992). *Personality and peer influence in juvenile corrections*. Westport, CT: Greenwood Press.

Goleman, D. (2006). *Social intelligence: The new science of human relationships*. New York: Bantam.

Golinkoff, R. M., & Hirsh-Pasek, K. (2016). *Becoming brilliant: What science tells us about raising successful children*. Washington, DC: American Psychological Association.

Gone, J. P. (2007). "We never was happy living like a Whiteman": Mental health disparities and the postcolonial predicament in American Indian communities. *American Journal of Community Psychology, 40*(3–4), 290–300.

Gone, J. P. (2015). Reconciling evidence-based practice and cultural competence in mental health services: Introduction to a special issue. *Transcultural Psychiatry, 52*(2), 139–149.

Gorman, M. J. (2018). *Samuel Beckett: Original manuscript drafts of Worstward Ho*. Dublin, Ireland: Science Gallery Dublin. Accessed at https://dublin .sciencegallery.com/failbetter/worstwardho on January 4, 2019.

Gottman, J. M. (2011). *The science of trust: Emotional attunement for couples*. New York: Norton.

Graff, J. (Ed.). (1987). Strength within the circle. *Journal of Child and Youth Care*. Accessed at www.cyc-net.org/journals/jcyc/jcycSpecial1987.html on January 7, 2019.

Grandjean, P., & Landrigan, P. J. (2014). Neurobehavioural effects of developmental toxicity. *Lancet Neurology, 13*(3), 330–338.

Gray, L. (2011). *First Nations 101*. Vancouver, Canada: Adaawx.

Gray, P. (2013). *Free to learn: Why unleashing the instinct to play will make our children happier, more self-reliant, and better students for life*. New York: Basic Books.

Greenleaf, R. K. (2002). *Servant leadership: A journey into the nature of legitimate power and greatness*. Mahwah, NJ: Paulist Press.

Greenwald, R. (2005). *Child trauma handbook: A guide for helping trauma-exposed children and adolescents*. New York: Haworth.

Griffin, K. R. (2008). *Use of cooperative learning and computer assisted instruction to investigate mathematics achievement scores, student's attitude toward cooperative learning and confidence in subject matter* (Doctoral dissertation), Duquesne University, Pittsburgh, PA.

Guthrie, J. W., & Schuermann, P. (2011). *Leading schools to success: Constructing and sustaining high-performing learning cultures*. Thousand Oaks, CA: SAGE.

Hafen, C. A., Allen, J. P., Mikami, A. Y., Gregory, A., Hamre, B., & Pianta, R. C. (2012). The pivotal role of adolescent autonomy in secondary school classrooms. *Journal of Youth and Adolescence, 41*(3), 245–255.

Hahn, K. (1959). *Dr. Kurt Hahn at the forty-eighth annual dinner of Old Centralians*. Accessed at www.kurthahn.org/wp-content/uploads/2017/02/2017 -oldcentral.pdf on January 7, 2019.

Haines, E. M. (1888). *The American Indian*. Chicago: Mas-sin-na-gan.

Hall, G. S. (1904). *Adolescence* (Vols. 1 and 2). New York: Appleton.

Hall, S. R. (1829). *Lectures on school-keeping*. Boston: Richardson, Lord and Holbrook.

Hall, S. S. (2012). Hidden treasures in junk DNA. *Scientific American, 307*(4). Accessed at www.scientificamerican.com/article/hidden-treasures-in-junk -dna on January 7, 2019.

Hallahan, D. P., Kauffman, J. M., & Pullen, P. C. (2013). *Exceptional learners: An introduction to special education* (13th ed.). New York: Pearson.

Hanushek, E. A., & Raymond, M. E. (2005). Does school accountability lead to improved school performance? *Journal of Policy Analysis and Management, 24*(2), 297–327.

Hardy, K. V. (2013). Healing the hidden wounds of racial trauma. *Reclaiming Children and Youth, 22*(1), 24–28.

Hassrick, R. B. (1964). *The Sioux: Life and customs of a warrior society.* Norman, OK: University of Oklahoma Press.

Hemingway, E. (1929). *A farewell to arms.* New York: Scribner's Sons.

Henggeler, S. W., Schoenwald, S. K., Borduin, C. M., Rowland, M. D., & Cunningham, P. B. (1998). *Multisystemic treatment of antisocial behavior in children and adolescents.* New York: Guilford Press.

Hernandez, P. (2016). *The pedagogy of real talk: Engaging, teaching, and connecting with students at risk.* Thousand Oaks, CA: Corwin Press.

Hibbing, J. R., Smith, K. B., & Alford, J. R. (2014). Differences in negativity bias underlie variations in political ideology. *Behavioral and Brain Sciences, 37*(3), 297–307.

Hobbs, N. (1994). *The troubled and troubling child.* Cleveland, OH: American Re-Education Association.

Hoffman, E. (1988). *The right to be human: A biography of Abraham Maslow.* Los Angeles: Tarcher.

Hoffman, M. L. (2000). *Empathy and moral development: Implications for caring and justice.* New York: Cambridge University Press.

Holman, H. (1908). *Pestalozzi: An account of his life and work.* Whitefish, MT: Kessinger.

Jackson, W. C. (2014). *The Circle of Courage: Childhood socialization in the 21st century* (Doctoral dissertation), Wayne State University, Detroit, MI.

James, A. B., & Lunday, T. (2014). Native birthrights and Indigenous science. *Reclaiming Children and Youth, 22*(4), 56–58.

James, S. (2011). What works in group care? A structured review of treatment models for group homes and residential care. *Children and Youth Services Review, 33*(2), 308–321.

James, W. (1984). The moral equivalent of war. In B. W. Wilshire (Ed.), *William James: The essential writings* (pp. 349–361). Albany, NY: State University of New York Press.

Janak, P. H., & Tye, K. M. (2015). From circuits to behaviour in the amygdala. *Nature, 15*(517), 284–293.

Jensen, E. (2019). *Poor students, rich teaching: Seven high-impact mindsets for students from poverty* (Rev. ed.). Bloomington, IN: Solution Tree Press.

Jigsaw Classroom. (n.d.). *History of the jigsaw: An account from Professor Aronson.* Accessed at www.jigsaw.org/history on February 21, 2019.

Johansen, B. E. (1998). *Debating democracy: Native American legacy of freedom.* Santa Fe, NM: Clear Light.

Johansen, T. K. (2012). *The powers of Aristotle's soul.* Oxford, England: Oxford University Press.

Johnson, L. A. (2006). *A toolbox for humanity: More than 9000 years of thought.* Bloomington, IN: Trafford.

Johnson, R. T., Johnson, D. W., & Stanne, M. B. (1986). Comparison of computer-assisted cooperative, competitive, and individualistic learning. *American Educational Research Journal, 23*(3), 382–392.

Juvonen, J., & Graham, S. (2013). Bullying in schools: The power of bullies and the plight of victims. *Annual Review of Psychology, 65*(1), 159–185.

Kagan, J. (1971). *Personality development.* New York: Harcourt Brace.

Kaye, C. B. (2010). *The complete guide to service learning: Proven, practical ways to engage students in civic responsibility, academic curriculum, and social action* (2nd ed.). Minneapolis, MN: Free Spirit.

Keller, H., & Kärtner, J. (2013). The cultural solution of universal developmental tasks. In M. J. Gelfand, C.-Y. Chiu, & Y.-Y. Hong (Eds.), *Advances in culture and psychology* (Vol. 3, pp. 63–116). New York: Oxford University Press.

Keltner, D. (2009). *Born to be good: The science of a meaningful life.* New York: Norton.

Keltner, D. (2016). *The power paradox: How we gain and lose influence.* New York: Penguin.

Keoke, E. D., & Porterfield, K. M. (2002). *Encyclopedia of American Indian contributions to the world.* New York: Facts on File.

Key, E. (1909). *Barnets århundrade* [*The century of the child*]. London: Putnam's Sons.

Kielsmeier, J. C., Scales, P. C., Roehlkepartain, E. C., & Neal, M. (2004). Community service and service-learning in public schools. *Reclaiming Children and Youth, 13*(3), 139–143.

Kirmayer, L. J., Gone, J. P., & Moses, J. (2014). Rethinking historical trauma. *Transcultural Psychiatry, 51*(3), 299–319.

Koehler, N., & Seger, V. (2011). The CLEAR problem-solving model: Discovering strengths and solutions. *Reclaiming Children and Youth, 20*(1), 16–19.

Kohn, A. (2015). *Schooling beyond measure and other unorthodox essays about education.* Portsmouth, NH: Heinemann.

Kohn, A. (2018). *Punished by rewards: The trouble with gold stars, incentive plans, A's, praise, and other bribes* (25th anniversary ed.). New York: Mariner Books.

Kolb, A. Y., & Kolb, D. A. (2017). *The experiential educator: Principles and practices of experiential learning.* Kaunakakai, HI: Experience Based Learning Systems.

Koltko-Rivera, M. E. (2006). Rediscovering the later version of Maslow's hierarchy of needs: Self-transcendence and opportunities for theory, research, and unification. *Review of General Psychology, 10*(2), 302–317.

Korczak, J. (1967). *Selected works of Janusz Korczak.* Washington, DC: National Science Foundation. Accessed at www.januszkorczak.ca/legacy /CombinedMaterials.pdf on January 7, 2019.

Korczak, J. (1986). *King Matt the first* (R. Lourie, Trans.). New York: Farrar, Straus and Giroux.

Kress, C. (2014). Transformational education: The 4-H legacy. *Reclaiming Children and Youth, 23*(3), 5–9.

Krisberg, B. (2005). *Juvenile justice: Redeeming our children.* San Francisco: SAGE.

Lane, H. (1975). *The wild boy of Aveyron.* Cambridge, MA: Harvard University Press.

Lantieri, L. (2001). An ounce of prevention is worth a pound of metal detectors. *Reclaiming Children and Youth, 10*(1), 33–38.

Lantieri, L. (2014). *Building emotional intelligence: Practices to cultivate inner resilience in children.* Louisville, CO: Sounds True.

Larson, S., & Brendtro, L. K. (2000). *Reclaiming our prodigal sons and daughters: A practical approach for connecting with youth in conflict.* Bloomington, IN: Solution Tree Press.

Laursen, E. K. (2010). The evidence base for positive peer culture. *Reclaiming Children and Youth, 19*(2), 37–43.

Laursen, E. K. (2018). *Intentional responsive adult practices: Supporting kids to not only overcome adversity but to thrive.* Morrisville, NC: Lulu.

Laursen, E. K., & Tate, T. F. (2012). Democratic group work. *Reclaiming Children and Youth, 20*(4), 46–51.

Lerner, R. M., Lerner, J. V., & colleagues. (2013, December). *The positive development of youth: Comprehensive findings from the 4-H study of positive youth development.* Medford, MA: Tufts University Institute for Applied Research in Youth Development.

Lewin, K. (1999). *The complete social scientist: A Kurt Lewin reader* (M. Gold, Ed.). Washington, DC: American Psychological Association.

Li, J., & Julian, M. M. (2012). Developmental relationships as the active ingredient: A unifying working hypothesis of "what works" across intervention settings. *American Journal of Orthopsychiatry, 82*(2), 156–167.

Long, N. J. (2014). Disengaging from conflict cycles. *Reclaiming Children and Youth, 23*(1), 34–37.

Long, N. J. (2015). Perspectives on conflict in the classroom after fifty years. *Reclaiming Children and Youth, 24*(1), 9–15.

Long, N. J., Wood, M. M., & Fecser, F. A. (2001). *Life Space Crisis Intervention: Talking with students in conflict* (2nd ed.). Austin, TX: Pro-Ed.

Longhurst, J., & McCord, J. (2014). Hooked on helping. *Reclaiming Children and Youth, 23*(1), 14–16.

Luthar, S. S. (2006). Resilience in development: A synthesis of research across five decades. In D. Cicchetti & D. J. Cohen (Eds.), *Developmental psychopathology: Risk, disorder, and adaption* (2nd ed., Vol. 3, pp. 739–795). Hoboken, NJ: Wiley.

Maier, H. W. (1982). To be attached and free: The challenge of child development in the eighties. *Child Welfare, 61*(2), 67–76.

Makarenko, A. S. (1951). *The road to life: An epic of education.* Moscow, Russia: Foreign Languages.

Marty, M. E. (1987). *Religion and republic: The American circumstance.* Boston: Beacon Press.

Maslow, A. H. (1943). A theory of human motivation. *Psychological Review, 50*, 370–396.

Maslow, A. H. (1959). Psychological data and value theory. In A. H. Maslow (Ed.), *New knowledge in human values* (pp. 119–136). New York: Harper & Row.

Maslow, A. H. (1970). *Motivation and personality*. New York: Harper & Row.

Masten, A. S. (2014). *Ordinary magic: Resilience in development*. New York: Guilford Press.

McCall, H. J. (2003). When successful alternative students "disengage" from regular school. *Reclaiming Children and Youth, 12*(2), 113–117.

McDonald, T. (2013). *Classroom management: Engaging students in learning*. Victoria, Australia: Oxford University Press.

McEwen, B. S. (2008). Understanding the potency of stressful early life experiences on brain and body function. *Metabolism, 57*(2), S11–S15.

McNulty, R. J., & Quaglia, R. J. (2007). Rigor, relevance and relationships. *School Administrator, 64*(8), 18–23.

Meaney, M. J. (2001). Maternal care, gene expression, and the transmission of individual differences in stress reactivity across generations. *Annual Review of Neuroscience, 24*(1), 1161–1192.

Menninger, K. (1963). *The vital balance: The life process in mental health and illness*. New York: Viking.

Menninger, K. (1982). The church's responsibility for the homeless. In R. Gillogly (Ed.), *Sacred shelters* (pp. 54–62). Topeka, KS: Villages.

Messerli, J. (1972). *Horace Mann: A biography*. New York: Knopf.

Mill, J. S. (2002). *The basic writings of John Stuart Mill: On liberty, the subjection of women and utilitarianism*. New York: Modern Library.

Milliken, B. (2007). *The last dropout: Stop the epidemic!* Carlsbad, CA: Hay House.

Modgil, S., & Modgil, C. (Eds.). (2015). *Lawrence Kohlberg: Consensus and controversy*. New York: Routledge.

Montessori, M. (1949). *The San Remo lectures*. Amsterdam, Netherlands: Association Montessori Internationale.

Montessori, M. (1967). *The absorbent mind*. New York: Houghton Mifflin.

Montessori, M. (2003). *The Montessori method*. Scotts Valley, CA: CreateSpace.

Morse, W. C. (2008). *Connecting with kids in conflict: A life space legacy*. Lennox, SD: Reclaiming Children and Youth.

Murphy, L. B., & Moriarty, A. E. (1976). *Vulnerability, coping, and growth: From infancy to adolescence*. New Haven, CT: Yale University Press.

National Archives. (n.d.) *Declaration of Independence: A transcription.* Accessed at www.archives.gov/founding-docs/declaration-transcript on March 21, 2019.

Nelson, C. A., Fox, N. A., & Zeanah, C. H. (2014). *Romania's abandoned children: Deprivation, brain development, and the struggle for recovery.* Cambridge, MA: Harvard University Press.

Neufeld, G., & Maté, G. (2005). *Hold on to your kids: Why parents need to matter more than peers.* New York: Ballantine Books.

Nicholls, J. G. (1992). What is ability and why are we mindful of it? A developmental perspective. In R. J. Sternberg & J. Kolligian Jr. (Eds.), *Competence considered* (pp. 11–40). New Haven, CT: Yale University Press.

Nichols, S. L., & Berliner, D. C. (2007). *Collateral damage: How high-stakes testing corrupts America's schools.* Cambridge, MA: Harvard Education Press.

Noddings, N. (2013). *Caring: A relational approach to ethics and moral education* (2nd ed.). Berkeley, CA: University of California Press.

Novak, S., & Slattery, C. (2018). *Deep discourse: Facilitating student-led discussions* [Video]. Bloomington, IN: Solution Tree Press.

Obomsawin, A. (Producer/Director), Canell, M. (Producer), & Verrall, R. (Producer). (1987). *Richard Cardinal: Cry from a diary of a Métis child* [Motion picture]. Montreal, Canada: National Film Board of Canada.

Odney, J., & Brendtro, L. K. (1992). Students grade their schools. *Journal of Emotional and Behavioral Problems, 1*(2), 4–9.

Olweus, D. (1993). *Bullying at school: What we know and what we can do.* New York: Wiley-Blackwell.

Osher, D., & Berg, J. (2018, January). *School climate and social and emotional learning: The integration of two approaches.* University Park, PA: Edna Bennett Pierce Prevention Research Center, Pennsylvania State University. Accessed at www.air.org/sites/default/files/downloads/report/School-Climate-and-Social-and-Emotional-Learning-Integrative-Approach-January-2018.pdf on January 7, 2019.

Owens, R. G., Jr., & Valesky, T. C. (2014). *Organizational behavior in education: Leadership and school reform* (11th ed.). New York: Allyn & Bacon.

Panksepp, J., & Biven, L. (2012). *The archaeology of mind: Neuroevolutionary origins of human emotions.* New York: Norton.

Parker, D. (2019). *Building bridges: Engaging students at risk through the power of relationships.* Bloomington, IN: Solution Tree Press.

Payne, W. H. (1875). *Chapters on school supervision: A practical treatise on superintendence; grading; arranging courses of study; the preparation and use of blanks, records, and reports; examinations for promotion.* Cincinnati, OH: Wilson, Hinkle.

Pember, M. A. (2017, October 3). Trauma may be woven into DNA of Native Americans. *Indian Country Today.* Accessed at https://newsmaven.io /indiancountrytoday/archive/trauma-may-be-woven-into-dna-of-native -americans-CbiAxpzar0WkMALhjrcGVQ on January 7, 2019.

Perry, B. D. (2001). *Bonding and attachment in maltreated children: Consequences of emotional neglect in childhood.* Accessed at https://childtrauma.org /wp-content/uploads/2013/11/Bonding_13.pdf on April 16, 2019.

Perry, B. D., & Hambrick, E. P. (2008). The neurosequential model of therapeutics. *Reclaiming Children and Youth, 17*(3), 39–43.

Perry, B. D., & Szalavitz, M. (2010). *Born for love: Why empathy is essential— and endangered.* New York: Morrow.

Perry, B. D., & Szalavitz, M. (2017). *The boy who was raised as a dog: And other stories from a child psychiatrist's notebook—What traumatized children can teach us about loss, love, and healing* (Rev. ed.). New York: Basic Books.

Peter, V. J. (2000). *What makes Boys Town successful? A description of the 21st century Boys Town teaching model.* Omaha, NE: Boys Town Press.

Peterson, C. (2013). The strengths revolution: A positive psychology perspective. *Reclaiming Children and Youth, 21*(4), 7–14.

Phelan, J. (2004). Some thoughts on using an ecosystem perspective. *CYC-Online, 68.* Accessed at www.cyc-net.org/cyc-online/cycol-0904-phelan .html on January 7, 2019.

Pihama, L., & Cameron, N. D. (2012). Kua tupu te pā harakeke: Developing healthy whānau relationships. In Waziyatawin & M. Yellow Bird (Eds.), *For Indigenous minds only: A decolonization handbook* (pp. 225–244). Santa Fe, NM: School for Advanced Research Press.

Pink, D. H. (2009). *Drive: The surprising truth about what motivates us.* New York: Riverhead Books.

Pluess, M., & Belsky, J. (2015). Vantage sensitivity: Genetic susceptibility to effects of positive experiences. In M. Pluess (Ed.), *Genetics of psychological well-being: The role of heritability and genetics in positive psychology* (pp. 193–210). Oxford, England: Oxford University Press.

Porges, S. W. (2018). Polyvagal theory: A primer. In S. W. Porges & D. Dana (Eds.), *Clinical applications of the polyvagal theory: The emergence of polyvagal-informed therapies* (pp. 50–69). New York: Norton.

Project Förderende. (2017, November 27). Presentation on positive peer culture by youth from Adelsheim Prison, Creglingen, Germany.

Prouty, D., Panicucci, J., & Collinson, R. (Eds.). (2007). *Adventure education: Theory and applications*. Champaign, IL: Human Kinetics.

Purvis, K. B., Cross, D. R., & Lyons-Sunshine, W. (2007). *The connected child: Bring hope and healing to your adoptive family*. New York: McGraw-Hill.

Putnam, R. D. (2000). *Bowling alone: The collapse and revival of American community*. New York: Simon & Schuster.

Quigley, R. (2014). Empowering our children to succeed. *Reclaiming Children and Youth, 23*(1), 24–27.

Redl, F., & Wineman, D. (1952). *Controls from within: Techniques for the treatment of the aggressive child*. New York: Free Press.

Reyhner, J., & Eder, J. (2006). *American Indian education: A history*. Norman, OK: University of Oklahoma Press.

Reyna, V. F., Chapman, S. B., Dougherty, M. R., & Confrey, J. (Eds.). (2012). *The adolescent brain: Learning, reasoning, and decision making*. Washington, DC: American Psychological Association.

Roediger, H. L., McDermott, K. B., & McDaniel, M. A. (2011). Using testing to improve learning and memory. In M. Gernsbacher, R. Pew, L. Hough, & J. R. Pomerantz (Eds.), *Psychology and the real world: Essays illustrating fundamental contributions to society* (pp. 69–78). New York: Worth.

Roehlkepartain, E. C., King, P. E., Wagener, L., & Benson, P. L. (2006). *Handbook of spiritual development in childhood and adolescence*. New York: SAGE.

Roehlkepartain, E. C., & Scales, P. C. (2007). *Developmental assets: A framework for enriching service-learning*. Minneapolis, MN: Search Institute. Accessed at www.search-institute.org/wp-content/uploads/2018/02/2007-Roehlkepartain -Assets-SL-NSLC.pdf on January 7, 2019.

Rogoff, B. (2003). *The cultural nature of human development*. New York: Oxford University Press.

Rogoff, B., Mejía-Arauz, R., & Correa-Chávez, M. (2015). A cultural paradigm: Learning by observing and pitching in. In M. Correa-Chávez, R. Mejía-Arauz, & B. Rogoff (Eds.), *Children learn by observing and contributing to family and community endeavors: A cultural paradigm* (Vol. 49, pp. 1–24). Waltham, MA: Academic Press.

Ross, R. (2009). *Dancing with a ghost: Exploring Indian reality*. New York: Penguin Global.

Rousseau, J.-J. (1979). *Emile: Or, on education* (A. Bloom, Trans.). New York: Basic Books.

Rutter, M. (2012). Resilience as a dynamic concept. *Development and Psychopathology, 24*(2), 335–344.

Rutter, M., O'Connor, T. G., & English and Romanian Adoptees (ERA) Study Team. (2004). Are there biological programming effects for psychological development? Findings from a study of Romanian adoptees. *Developmental Psychology, 40*(1), 81–94.

Ryan, R. M., & Deci, E. L. (2017). *Self-determination theory: Basic psychological needs in motivation, development, and wellness*. New York: Guilford Press.

Schunk, D. H. (1991). Self-efficacy and academic motivation. *Educational Psychologist, 26*(3–4), 207–231. Accessed at http://libres.uncg.edu/ir/uncg/f/D_Schunk_Self_1991.pdf on January 7, 2019.

Scott, E. S., & Steinberg, L. (2008). *Rethinking juvenile justice*. Cambridge, MA: Harvard University Press.

Seita, J. R. (2012). Reclaiming family privilege. *Reclaiming Children and Youth, 21*(2), 34–39.

Seita, J. R. (2014). Family privilege. *Reclaiming Children and Youth, 23*(2), 7–12.

Seita, J. R., & Brendtro, L. K. (2005). *Kids who outwit adults*. Bloomington, IN: Solution Tree Press.

Seligman, M. E. P. (2011). *Flourish: A visionary new understanding of happiness and well-being*. New York: Free Press.

Selye, H. (1974). *Stress without distress*. Philadelphia: Lippincott.

Shapin, S. (1998). *The scientific revolution*. Chicago: University of Chicago Press.

Shapiro, F. R. (Ed.). (2006). *The Yale book of quotations*. New Haven, CT: Yale University Press.

Shareski, D. (2017). *Embracing a culture of joy*. Bloomington, IN: Solution Tree Press.

Siegel, D. J. (2010). *Mindsight: The new science of personal transformation*. New York: Bantam Books.

Siegel, D. J. (2012). *The developing mind: How relationships and the brain interact to shape who we are*. New York: Guilford Press.

Siegel, D. J. (2015). *Brainstorm: The power and purpose of the teenage brain.* New York: Penguin.

Slavin, R. E. (1995). *Cooperative learning: Theory, research, and practice* (2nd ed.). Boston: Allyn & Bacon.

Slavin, R. E. (2005, March). *Evidence-based reform: Advancing the education of students at risk.* Washington, DC: Center for American Progress. Accessed at www.americanprogress.org/wp-content/uploads/kf/Slavin%203%2017%20FINAL.pdf on January 7, 2019.

Slavin, R. E., Hurley, E. A., & Chamberlain, A. M. (2003). Cooperative learning and achievement: Theory and research. In W. M. Reynolds & G. E. Miller (Eds.), *Handbook of psychology* (Vol. 7, pp. 177–198). Hoboken, NJ: Wiley.

Slavson, S. R. (1965). *Reclaiming the delinquent by para-analytic group psychotherapy and the inversion technique.* New York: Free Press.

Smith, M. (2009). *Rethinking residential child care: Positive perspectives.* Bristol, England: Policy Press.

Sneve, V. D. H. (1998). *Completing the circle.* Lincoln, NE: University of Nebraska Press.

Spencer, H. (1864). *The principles of biology* (Vol. 1). London: Williams and Norgate.

Sroufe, L. A., Egeland, B., Carlson, E. A., & Collins, W. A. (2005). *The development of the person: The Minnesota study of risk and adaptation from birth to adulthood.* New York: Guilford Press.

Stack Exchange. (n.d.) *English language & usage: Origin of "I hear and I forget. I see and I remember. I do and I understand."?* Accessed at https://english .stackexchange.com/questions/226886/origin-of-i-hear-and-i-forget-i-see -and-i-remember-i-do-and-i-understand on April 16, 2019.

Standing Bear, L. (2006). *Land of the spotted eagle* (New ed.). Lincoln, NE: University of Nebraska Press.

Steinberg, L. (2014). *Age of opportunity: Lessons from the new science of adolescence.* Boston: Houghton Mifflin Harcourt.

Sternberg, R. (1996). *Successful intelligence: How practical and creative intelligence predicts success in life.* New York: Plume.

Stobaugh, R. (2019). *Fifty strategies to boost cognitive engagement: Creating a thinking culture in the classroom.* Bloomington, IN: Solution Tree Press.

Stott, D. (1982). *Delinquency: The problem and its prevention*. New York: SP Medical and Scientific Books.

Strother, M. A. (2007). A mind for adventure. *Reclaiming Children and Youth, 16*(1), 17–21.

Sue, D. W. (2010). *Microaggressions in everyday life: Race, gender, and sexual orientation*. New York: Wiley.

Sugai, G., & Horner, R. (2009). Defining and describing schoolwide positive behavior support. In W. Sailor, G. Dunlap, G. Sugai, & R. Horner (Eds.), *Handbook of positive behavior support* (pp. 307–326). New York: Springer.

Sugden, K., Arseneault, L., Harrington, H., Moffitt, T. E., Williams, B., & Caspi, A. (2010). The serotonin transporter gene moderates the development of emotional problems among children following bullying victimization. *Journal of the American Academy of Child and Adolescent Psychiatry, 49*(8), 830–840.

Sylwester, R. (2005). *How to explain a brain: An educator's handbook of brain terms and cognitive processes*. Thousand Oaks, CA: Corwin Press.

Szalavitz, M., & Perry, B. D. (2010). *Born for love: Why empathy is essential— and endangered*. New York: Morrow.

Szyf, M., McGowan, P. O., Turecki, G., & Meaney, M. J. (2010). The social environment and the epigenome. In C. M. Worthman, P. M. Plotsky, D. S. Schechter, & C. A. Cummings (Eds.), *Formative experiences: The interaction of caregiving, culture, and developmental psychobiology* (pp. 53–81). New York: Cambridge University Press.

Tam, B. Y., Findlay, L. C., & Kohen, D. E. (2017). Indigenous families: Who do you call family? *Journal of Family Studies, 23*(3), 243–259.

Tate, T., Copas, R., & Wasmund, W. (2012). *Partners in empowerment: A practitioner's guide to implementing peer group treatment models*. Albion, MI: Starr Commonwealth.

Taylor, S. E. (2002). *The tending instinct: How nurturing is essential for who we are and how we live*. New York: Holt.

Terence. (2006). *The comedies* (P. Brown, Trans.). New York: Oxford University Press.

Tillich, P. (1952). *The courage to be*. New Haven, CT: Yale University Press.

Tooby, J., & Cosmides, L. (1990). On the universality of human nature and the uniqueness of the individual: The role of genetics and adaptation. *Journal of Personality, 58*(1), 17–67.

Tragaskis, S. (2015, May 15). 50 years later, recalling a founder of Head Start. *Cornell Chronicle.* Accessed at http://news.cornell.edu/stories/2015/05/50 -years-later-recalling-founder-head-start on May 31, 2019.

Treasurer, B. (2003). *Right risk: 10 powerful principles for taking giant leaps with your life.* Oakland, CA: Berrett-Koehler.

Tully, F., & Brendtro, L. K. (1998). Reaching angry and unattached kids. *Reclaiming Children and Youth, 7*(3), 147–154.

Turkle, S. (2017). *Alone together: Why we expect more from technology and less from each other* (Rev. ed.). New York: Basic Books.

Turnbull, A. P., Turbiville, V., & Turnbull, H. R. (2000). Evolution of family– professional partnerships: Collective empowerment as the model for the early twenty-first century. In J. P. Shonkoff & S. J. Meisels (Eds.), *Handbook of early childhood intervention* (2nd ed., pp. 630–650). New York: Cambridge University Press.

U.S. Department of Education. (2010). *Implementation blueprint and self-assessment: Positive behavioral interventions and supports.* Accessed at www.pbis .org/Common/Cms/files/pbisresources/SWPBS_ImplementationBlueprint _vSep_23_2010.pdf on January 7, 2019.

Van Bockern, S. (2018). *Schools that matter: Teaching the mind, reaching the heart.* Winnipeg, Manitoba: University of Winnipeg Faculty of Education.

van der Kolk, B. (2007). The complexity of adaptation to trauma: Self-regulation, stimulus discrimination, and characterological development. In B. van der Kolk, A. C. McFarlane, & L. Weisaeth (Eds.), *Traumatic stress: The effects of overwhelming experience on mind, body, and society* (pp. 182–213). New York: Guilford Press.

van der Kolk, B. (2014). *The body keeps the score: Mind, brain and body in the transformation of trauma.* New York: Viking.

Vilakazi, H. (1993). Rediscovering lost truths. *Journal of Emotional and Behavioral Problems, 1*(4), 37.

Vorrath, H. H., & Brendtro, L. K. (1985). *Positive peer culture* (2nd ed.). New York: Routledge.

Walker, J. R. (1982). *Lakota society* (R. J. DeMallie, Ed.). Lincoln, NE: University of Nebraska Press.

Walker, T. D. (2017). *Teach like Finland: 33 simple strategies for joyful classrooms.* New York: Norton.

Wallach, M., & Wallach, L. (1983). *Psychology's sanction for selfishness: The error of egoism in theory and therapy.* New York: Freeman.

Watanabe-Crockett, L. (2019). *Future-focused learning: 10 essential shifts of everyday practice.* Bloomington, IN: Solution Tree Press.

Werner, E. E. (2012). Risk, resilience, and recovery [Interview]. *Reclaiming Children and Youth, 21*(1), 18–23.

Werner, E. E., & Smith, R. S. (1977). *Kauai's children come of age.* Honolulu, HI: University of Hawaii Press.

Werner, E. E., & Smith, R. S. (1982). *Vulnerable but invincible: A longitudinal study of resilient children and youth.* New York: McGraw-Hill.

Werner, E. E., & Smith, R. S. (1992). *Overcoming the odds: High risk children from birth to adulthood.* Ithaca, NY: Cornell University Press.

Werner, E. E., & Smith, R. S. (2001). *Journeys from childhood to midlife: Risk, resilience, and recovery.* Ithaca, NY: Cornell University Press.

Werry, J. (2013). Fifty years in child and adolescent psychiatry. *Reclaiming Children and Youth, 22*(2), 25–30.

Whelan, R. J. (Ed.). (1998). *Emotional and behavioral disorders: A 25-year focus.* Denver, CO: Love.

Whewell, W. (1847). *The philosophy of the inductive sciences.* London: Parker.

White, R. W. (1959). Motivation reconsidered: The concept of competence. *Psychological Review, 66*(5), 297–333.

Whitney, S. (2015, August 21). Does George Blue Bird deserve freedom? *Argus Leader.* Accessed at www.argusleader.com/story/news/columnists /stu-whitney/2015/08/21/george-blue-bird-lakota-manslaughter-prison -native-stu-whitney/32137615 on January 7, 2019.

Wilker, K. (1993). *Der Lindenhof* (S. Lhotzky, Trans.). Sioux Falls, SD: Augustana University.

Wilkinson, R., & Pickett, K. (2011). *The spirit level: Why greater equality makes societies stronger.* New York: Bloomsbury Press.

Wills, W. D. (1941). *The Hawkspur experiment: An informal account of the training of wayward adolescents.* London: Allen & Unwin.

Wilson, E. O. (1998). *Consilience: The unity of knowledge.* New York: Knopf.

Wilson, L. (2012). *Steve Biko.* Athens, OH: Ohio University Press.

Wolins, M., & Wozner, Y. (1982). *Revitalizing residential settings*. San Francisco: Jossey-Bass.

Woods, D. (2017). *Biko: The powerful biography of Steve Biko and the struggle of the Black Consciousness Movement*. London: Endeavour Press.

Zedelius, C. M., Müller, B. C. N., & Schooler, J. W. (Eds.). (2017). *The science of lay theories: How beliefs shape our cognition, behavior, and health*. New York: Springer.

Zeigarnik, B. (1927). Das Behalten erledigter und unerledigter Handlungen [The memory of completed and uncompleted tasks]. *Psychologische Forschung, 9*(1), 1–85.

Zimmers, P. J. (1918). *Teaching boys and girls how to study*. Madison, WI: Parker Education.

Zynga, A. (2014, May 6). A social brain is a smarter brain. *Harvard Business Review*. Accessed at http://hbr.org/2014/05/a-social-brain-is-a-smarter-brain on January 7, 2019.

Index

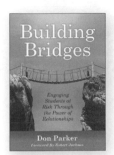

Building Bridges
Don Parker
Reach every learner by building teacher-student relationships and creating a welcoming learning environment that fosters motivation, engagement, and achievement.
BKF846

Every Student, Every Day
Kristyn Klei Borrero
Learn how to become a No-Nonsense Nurturer®— an educator who builds life-altering relationships with students and holds him- or herself and students accountable for achievement.
BKF843

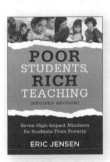

Poor Students, Rich Teaching, Revised Edition
Eric Jensen
The latest edition of *Poor Students, Rich Teaching* details seven essential mindsets for reaching students from poverty.
BKF887

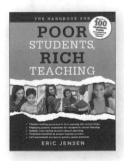

The Handbook for Poor Students, Rich Teaching
Eric Jensen
Discover a plethora of tools, organizers, worksheets, and surveys designed to help you change the lives of students from poverty.
BKF888

Wait! Your professional development journey doesn't have to end with the last pages of this book.

We realize improving student learning doesn't happen overnight. And your school or district shouldn't be left to puzzle out all the details of this process alone.

No matter where you are on the journey, we're committed to helping you get to the next stage.

Take advantage of everything from **custom workshops** to **keynote presentations** and **interactive web and video conferencing**. We can even help you develop an action plan tailored to fit your specific needs.

Let's get the conversation started.

Call 888.763.9045 today.